Warning disclaimer The following book is for entertainment and informational purposes only. The information presented is without contract or any type of guarantee assurance. While every caution has been taken to provide accurate and current information, it is solely the reader's responsibility to check all information contained in this article before relying upon it. Neither the author nor publisher can be held accountable for any errors or omissions. Under no circumstances will any legal responsibility or blame be held against the author or publisher for any reparation, damages, or monetary loss due to the information presented, either directly or indirectly. This book is not intended as legal or medical advice. If any such specialized advice is needed, seek a qualified individual for help.

Trademarks are used without permission. Use of the trademark is not authorized by, associated with, or sponsored by the trademark owners. All trademarks and brands used within this book are used with no intent to infringe on the trademark owners and only used for clarifying purposes.

Contents

YELLOW RICE WITH VEGETABLES

Servings: 6 | Prep: 15m | Cooks: 45m | Total: 45m

NUTRITION FACTS

Calories: 205.8 | Carbohydrates: 42.8g | Fat: g | Protein: 4.4g | Cholesterol: 0mg | Sodium: 1243.9mg

INGREDIENTS

- 1 teaspoon vegetable oil
- 1 small onion, chopped
- 1 carrot, diced
- 1/2 cup chopped broccoli florets
- 1/4 cup diced red bell pepper
- 1 clove garlic, minced
- 3 cups vegetable broth
- 1 1/2 cups rice
- 1 (1.41 ounce) package sazon seasoning with coriander and achiote (such as Goya)
- 1 dash adobo seasoning with pepper (such as Goya)

DIRECTIONS

1. Heat oil in a saucepan over medium heat. Cook and stir onion, carrot, broccoli, red bell pepper, and garlic in hot oil until garlic just begins to brown, about 5 minutes.
2. Pour vegetable broth into the saucepan; add rice, sazon seasoning, and adobo seasoning and stir. Bring the liquid to a boil, reduce heat to low, and cook until the liquid is absorbed and the rice is tender, about 25 minutes. Fluff rice with a fork to serve.

CASHEW RAISIN RICE PILAF

Servings: 12 | Prep: 15m | Cooks: 30m | Total: 45m

NUTRITION FACTS

Calories: 270.2 | Carbohydrates: 41.3g | Protein: 6.5g | Cholesterol: 0mg | Sodium: 346.4mg

INGREDIENTS

- 1/4 cup margarine
- 1 1/2 cups uncooked long grain white rice
- 1 chopped onion
- 3/4 cup uncooked wild rice
- 2 cups frozen green peas
- 1 (4 ounce) jar diced pimento peppers, drained

- 1 cup chopped carrot
- 1 cup golden raisins
- 3 cups chicken broth
- 1 cup cashews
- 1 teaspoon salt
- ground black pepper to taste

DIRECTIONS

1. Melt margarine in a large saucepan over medium-high heat. Saute the long grain rice, onion, carrot and raisins for 3 to 5 minutes or until onion is tender. Pour in the broth and bring to a boil. Reduce heat to low, cover pan and simmer for 20 to 25 minutes.
2. Meanwhile, in a saucepan bring 1 1/2 cups salted water to a boil. Add wild rice, reduce heat, cover and simmer for 45 minutes. Drain and set aside.
3. When the rice/raisin mixture is finished simmering (rice is cooked), stir in cooked wild rice, peas, pimentos and cashews and heat through.

BUTTERNUT SQUASH AND SHIITAKE MUSHROOM WILD RICE RISOTTO

Servings: 10 | Prep: 40m | Cooks: 1h | Total: 1h40m

NUTRITION FACTS

Calories: 400 | Carbohydrates: 64.6g | Fat: 10.2g | Protein: 9.1g | Cholesterol: 21mg | Sodium: 257mg

INGREDIENTS

- 3 ounces dried sliced shiitake mushrooms
- 4 cups water
- 4 cups cubed butternut squash
- 2 tablespoons olive oil
- 1 tablespoon maple syrup (optional)
- 4 cups vegetable stock
- 3 tablespoons butter
- 1 large onion, finely chopped
- 1 cup wild rice
- 2 cups Arborio rice
- 1 cup dry white wine
- 1 (4 ounce) container crumbled Gorgonzola cheese
- salt and ground black pepper to taste
- 1/2 cup chopped fresh flat-leaf parsley

DIRECTIONS

1. Combine the shiitake mushrooms and water in a bowl, assuring the mushrooms are covered with water; allow to soak until the mushrooms have softened, about 30 minutes. Drain and reserve the liquid for later use.
2. Preheat an oven to 375 degrees F (190 degrees C).
3. Toss the butternut squash, olive oil, and maple syrup together in a bowl until the squash is evenly coated. Spread onto a baking sheet.
4. Roast the squash in the preheated oven until tender yet retains its shape, about 30 minutes; set aside.
5. Bring the vegetable stock and the reserved liquid from the mushrooms to a simmer in a saucepan over medium heat.
6. Melt the butter in a large skillet over medium heat; when the butter begins to foam, stir the onion into the butter and cook until the onions are soft and golden, 5 to 7 minutes. Stir the wild rice and the Arborio rice through the onions until evenly mixed and coated. Add the white wine and mushrooms to the onion; cook, stirring occasionally, until the liquid has been absorbed, 7 to 10 minutes.
7. Pour enough of the simmering stock mixture into the skillet to cover the rice; cook and stir until the liquid is nearly completely absorbed. Continue adding stock about 3/4 cups at a time, allowing each batch to absorb into the mixture before adding the next. Cook and stir until the rice is tender, about 35 minutes total. Add the butternut squash; cook until the squash is hot, 2 to 3 minutes. Reduce heat to low. Quickly stir the Gorgonzola cheese and parsley into the mixture until the risotto is moist and creamy; remove from heat. Season with salt and pepper; serve immediately.

BROCCOLI RICE CASSEROLE

Servings: 10 | Prep: 30m | Cooks: 45m | Total: 1h15m

NUTRITION FACTS

Calories: 612.4 | Carbohydrates: 92.1g | Protein: 20.7g | Cholesterol: 47.3mg | Sodium: 1165.9mg

INGREDIENTS

- 2 (10 ounce) packages frozen chopped broccoli
- 3 cups instant rice
- 1 (10.75 ounce) can condensed cream of mushroom soup
- 1 (10.75 ounce) can condensed cream of chicken soup
- 1 1/4 cups water
- 1 (16 ounce) package processed American cheese, cubed
- 1 tablespoon butter
- 1 bunch celery, chopped
- 1 large onion, chopped
- 1 pinch salt and pepper to taste

DIRECTIONS

1. Cook broccoli and rice according to package directions. Preheat oven to 350 degrees F (175 degrees C).
2. In a medium saucepan over low heat, mix cream of mushroom soup, cream of chicken soup, and 1 1/4 cups water. Gradually stir in cheese until melted. Be careful that the cheese doesn't burn.
3. Melt butter in a large skillet over medium-high heat, and cook and stir celery and onion until soft.
4. In a large mixing bowl, combine broccoli, rice, soup and cheese mixture, celery and onion. Season with salt and pepper. Pour mixture into a 9x13 inch baking dish.
5. Bake in the preheated oven for 45 minutes, until bubbly and lightly brown.

HARVEST RICE DISH

Servings: 6 | Prep: 15m | Cooks: 1h30m | Total: 1h45m

NUTRITION FACTS

Calories: 278 | Carbohydrates: 42.7g | Fat: 11g | Protein: 5.4g | Cholesterol: 17mg | Sodium: 366mg

INGREDIENTS

- 1/2 cup slivered almonds
- 2 cups chicken broth
- 1/2 cup uncooked brown rice
- 1/2 cup uncooked wild rice
- 3 tablespoons butter
- 1 tablespoon brown sugar
- 1 cup dried cranberries
- 2/3 cup fresh sliced mushrooms
- 1/2 teaspoon orange zest

DIRECTIONS

1. Place almonds on an ungreased baking sheet. Toast at 350 degrees F (175 degrees C) for 5 to 8 minutes.
2. Mix broth, brown rice, and wild rice in a medium saucepan, and bring to boil. Reduce heat to low, cover, and simmer 45 minutes, until rice is tender and broth is absorbed.
3. In medium skillet, melt butter over medium-high heat. Add onions and brown sugar. Saute until butter is absorbed and onions are translucent and soft. Reduce heat, and cook onions for another 20 minutes, until they are caramelized.
4. Stir cranberries and mushrooms into the skillet. Cover, and cook 10 minutes or until berries start to swell. Stir in almonds and orange zest, then fold the mixture into the cooked rice. Salt and pepper to taste.

THE VERY BEST CONFETTI RICE

Servings: 8 | Prep: 10m | Cooks: 20m | Total: 35m | Additional: 5m

NUTRITION FACTS

Calories: 239 | Carbohydrates: 46.6g | Protein: 4.7g | Cholesterol: 0mg | Sodium: 5.3mg | Sodium: 5.3mg

INGREDIENTS

- 2 cups uncooked jasmine rice
- 4 cups water
- 1 tablespoon grated orange zest
- 1/2 cup dried cranberries
- 1/2 cup slivered almonds
- 1/2 cup sliced green onions

DIRECTIONS

1. Place the rice in a saucepan, and bring water to a boil over medium-high heat. Reduce the heat, cover, and simmer, about 20 minutes. Remove from heat and let sit about 5 minutes.
2. Stir the orange zest, cranberries, almonds, and green onions into the rice until blended.

SARAH'S RICE PILAF

Servings: 4 | Prep: 10m | Cooks: 35m | Total: 50m | Additional: 5m

NUTRITION FACTS

Calories: 244 | Carbohydrates: 40g | Protein: 5.9g | Cholesterol: 17.8mg | Sodium: 524.3mg

INGREDIENTS

- 2 tablespoons butter
- 1/2 cup orzo pasta
- 1/2 cup diced onion
- 2 cloves garlic, minced
- 1/2 cup uncooked white rice
- 2 cups chicken broth

DIRECTIONS

1. Melt the butter in a lidded skillet over medium-low heat. Cook and stir orzo pasta until golden brown. Stir in onion and cook until onion becomes translucent, then add garlic and cook for 1 minute. Mix in the rice and chicken broth. Increase heat to high and bring to a boil. Reduce heat to medium-low, cover, and simmer until the rice is tender, and the liquid has been absorbed, 20 to 25 minutes. Remove from heat and let stand for 5 minutes, then fluff with a fork.

LEMON BASMATI RICE

Servings: 4 | Prep: 10m | Cooks: 20m | Total: 30m

NUTRITION FACTS

Calories: 194 | Carbohydrates: 40.3g | Fat: 3g | Protein: 3.9g | Cholesterol: 0mg | Sodium: 1mg

INGREDIENTS

- 2 teaspoons canola oil
- 1 cup basmati rice, rinsed
- 1 (2 inch) piece fresh ginger, minced
- 1 lemon, juiced and zested
- 2 cups chicken broth
- salt and ground black pepper to taste

DIRECTIONS

1. Heat the oil in a pot over medium heat. Cook the rice, ginger, and lemon zest together in the hot oil for about 1 minute; add the lemon juice and chicken broth. Bring the mixture to a boil; cover the pot and allow the mixture to simmer until the liquid is absorbed and the rice is tender, 18 to 20 minutes. Season with salt and pepper.

MEXICAN RICE

Servings: 4 | Prep: 5m | Cooks: 25m | Total: 30m

NUTRITION FACTS

Calories: 291 | Carbohydrates: 42.2g | Protein: 4.8g | Cholesterol: 2.5mg | Sodium: 1095.6mg

INGREDIENTS

- 3 tablespoons vegetable oil
- 1 cup uncooked long-grain rice
- 1 teaspoon garlic salt
- 1/2 teaspoon ground cumin
- 1/4 cup chopped onion
- 1/2 cup tomato sauce
- 2 cups chicken broth

DIRECTIONS

1. Heat oil in a large saucepan over medium heat and add rice. Cook, stirring constantly, until puffed and golden. While rice is cooking, sprinkle with salt and cumin.

2. Stir in onions and cook until tender. Stir in tomato sauce and chicken broth; bring to a boil. Reduce heat to low, cover and simmer for 20 to 25 minutes. Fluff with a fork.

BEST SPANISH RICE

Servings: 5 | Prep: 10m | Cooks: 20m | Total: 30m

NUTRITION FACTS

Calories: 286 | Carbohydrates: 50.9g | Protein: 5.7g | Cholesterol: 2mg | Sodium: 696.6mg

INGREDIENTS

- 2 tablespoons oil
- 2 tablespoons chopped onion
- 1 1/2 cups uncooked white rice
- 2 cups chicken broth
- 1 cup chunky salsa

DIRECTIONS

1. Heat oil in a large, heavy skillet over medium heat. Stir in onion, and cook until tender, about 5 minutes.
2. Mix rice into skillet, stirring often. When rice begins to brown, stir in chicken broth and salsa. Reduce heat, cover and simmer 20 minutes, until liquid has been absorbed.

SPANISH RICE

Servings: 4 | Prep: 10m | Cooks: 30m | Total: 40m

NUTRITION FACTS

Calories: 269.7 | Carbohydrates: 45.7g | Protein: 4.8g | Cholesterol: 0mg | Sodium: 881.5mg

INGREDIENTS

- 2 tablespoons vegetable oil
- 1 cup uncooked white rice
- 1 onion, chopped
- 1/2 green bell pepper, chopped
- 2 cups water
- 1 (10 ounce) can diced tomatoes and green chiles
- 2 teaspoons chili powder, or to taste
- 1 teaspoon salt

DIRECTIONS

1. Heat oil in a deep skillet over medium heat. Saute rice, onion, and bell pepper until rice is browned and onions are tender.
2. Stir in water and tomatoes. Season with chili powder and salt. Cover, and simmer for 30 minutes, or until rice is cooked and liquid is absorbed.

MEXICAN RICE

Servings: 6 | Prep: 5m | Cooks: 25m | Total: 30m

NUTRITION FACTS

Calories: 158 | Carbohydrates: 29.1g | Protein: 3.4g | Cholesterol: 1.4mg | Sodium: 630.6mg

INGREDIENTS

- 1 cup long grain white rice
- 1 tablespoon vegetable oil
- 1 1/2 cups chicken broth
- 1/2 onion, finely chopped
- 1/2 green bell pepper, finely chopped
- 1 fresh jalapeno pepper, chopped
- 1 tomato, seeded and chopped
- 1 cube chicken bouillon
- 1/2 teaspoon salt and pepper to taste
- 1/2 teaspoon ground cumin
- 1/2 cup chopped fresh cilantro
- 1 clove garlic, halved

DIRECTIONS

1. In a medium sauce pan, cook rice in oil over medium heat for about 3 minutes. Pour in chicken broth, and bring to a boil. Stir in onion, green pepper, jalapeno, and diced tomato. Season with bouillon cube, salt and pepper, cumin, cilantro, and garlic. Bring to a boil, cover, and reduce heat to low. Cook for 20 minutes.

LIME CILANTRO RICE

Servings: 4 | Prep: 10m | Cooks: 20m | Total: 30m

NUTRITION FACTS

Calories: 84 | Carbohydrates: 12.7g | Fat: 3.1g | Protein: 2.4g | Cholesterol: 8mg | Sodium: 28mg

INGREDIENTS

- 2 cups water
- 1 tablespoon butter
- 1 cup long-grain white rice
- 1 teaspoon lime zest
- 2 tablespoons fresh lime juice
- 1/2 cup chopped cilantro

DIRECTIONS

1. Bring the water to a boil; stir the butter and rice into the water. Cover, reduce heat to low, and simmer until the rice is tender, about 20 minutes.
2. Stir the lime zest, lime juice, and cilantro into the cooked rice just before serving.

CARROT RICE

Servings: 6 | Prep: 15m | Cooks: 20m | Total: 35m

NUTRITION FACTS

Calories: 179 | Carbohydrates: 30.1g | Fat: 4.8g | Protein: 4g | Cholesterol: 0mg | Sodium: 34mg

INGREDIENTS

- 1 cup basmati rice
- 2 cups water
- 1/4 cup roasted peanuts
- 1 tablespoon margarine
- 1 onion, sliced
- 1 teaspoon minced fresh ginger root
- 3/4 cup grated carrots
- salt to taste
- cayenne pepper to taste
- chopped fresh cilantro

DIRECTIONS

1. Combine rice and water in a medium saucepan. Bring to a boil over high heat. Reduce heat to low, cover with lid, and allow to steam until tender, about 20 minutes.
2. While rice is cooking, grind peanuts in a blender and set aside. Heat the margarine in a skillet over medium heat. Stir in the onion; cook and stir until the onion has softened and turned golden brown about 10 minutes. Stir in ginger, carrots, and salt to taste. Reduce heat to low and cover to steam 5 minutes. Stir in cayenne pepper and peanuts. When rice is done, add it to skillet and stir gently to combine with other ingredients. Garnish with chopped cilantro.

ASPARAGUS CASHEW RICE PILAF
Servings: 8 | Prep: 25m | Cooks: 25m | Total: 50m

NUTRITION FACTS

Calories: 249 | Carbohydrates: 35.1g | Protein: 5.3g | Cholesterol: 15.3mg | Sodium: 172.1mg

INGREDIENTS

- 1/4 cup butter
- 2 ounces uncooked spaghetti, broken
- 1/4 cup minced onion
- 1/2 teaspoon minced garlic
- 1 1/4 cups uncooked jasmine rice
- 2 1/4 cups vegetable broth
- salt and pepper to taste
- 1/2 pound fresh asparagus, trimmed and cut into 2 inch pieces
- 1/2 cup cashew halves

DIRECTIONS

1. Melt butter in a medium saucepan over medium-low heat. Increase heat to medium, and stir in spaghetti, cooking until coated with the melted butter and lightly browned.
2. Stir onion and garlic into the saucepan, and cook about 2 minutes, until tender. Stir in jasmine rice, and cook about 5 minutes. Pour in vegetable broth. Season mixture with salt and pepper. Bring the mixture to a boil, cover, and cook 20 minutes, until rice is tender and liquid has been absorbed.
3. Place asparagus in a separate medium saucepan with enough water to cover. Bring to a boil, and cook until tender but firm.
4. Mix asparagus and cashew halves into the rice mixture, and serve warm.

MUSHROOM RICE
Servings: 4 | Prep: 5m | Cooks: 25m | Total: 30m

NUTRITION FACTS

Calories: 215.7 | Carbohydrates: 41.1g | Protein: 5.3g | Cholesterol: 8.4mg | Sodium: 1181.1mg

INGREDIENTS

- 2 teaspoons butter
- 6 mushrooms, coarsely chopped
- 2 cups chicken broth
- 1 cup uncooked white rice

- 1 clove garlic, minced
- 1 green onion, finely chopped
- 1/2 teaspoon chopped fresh parsley
- 1 teaspoon salt and pepper to taste

DIRECTIONS

1. Melt butter in a saucepan over medium heat. Cook mushrooms, garlic and green onion until mushrooms are cooked and liquid has evaporated. Stir in chicken broth and rice. Season with parsley, salt and pepper. Reduce heat, cover and simmer for 20 minutes.

ONION RICE

Servings: 6 | Prep: 10m | Cooks: 30m | Total: 40m

NUTRITION FACTS

Calories: 140.8 | Carbohydrates: 26.6g | Protein: 2.4g | Cholesterol: 0mg | Sodium: 2.4mg

INGREDIENTS

- 1 tablespoon vegetable oil
- 1 red onion, chopped
- 1 cup long-grain white rice
- 1 teaspoon ground black pepper
- 2 cups chicken broth

DIRECTIONS

1. Heat the oil in a saucepan over medium heat. Stir in the onion, and cook until almost tender. Stir in rice, and continue cooking until coated with oil. When onion is tender and rice begins to brown lightly, season with pepper, and pour in the broth. Bring to a boil. Reduce heat to low, cover, and simmer 20 minutes.

OVEN BROWN RICE

Servings: 8 | Prep: 10m | Cooks: 1h | Total: 1h10m

NUTRITION FACTS

Calories: 139.9 | Carbohydrates: 18.3g | Protein: 2.2g | Cholesterol: 15.3mg | Sodium: 481.6mg

INGREDIENTS

- 1 cup brown rice
- 1 cup beef broth
- 1 (14.5 ounce) can chicken broth

- 1/4 cup butter, melted
- 1 teaspoon garlic salt
- 1 teaspoon seasoned salt

DIRECTIONS

1. Preheat oven to 350 degrees F (175 degrees C).
2. In a 2 quart casserole dish, mix together rice, beef broth, chicken broth, butter, garlic salt, and seasoned salt. Bake uncovered in preheated oven for 60 minutes, until liquid is absorbed and rice is tender.

EASY MUSHROOM RICE

Servings: 4 | Prep: 5m | Cooks: 1h | Total: 1h5m

NUTRITION FACTS

Calories: 336.3 | Carbohydrates: 45.4g | Protein: 9.1g | Cholesterol: 33.4mg | Sodium: 1215.8mg

INGREDIENTS

- 1 cup uncooked long-grain rice
- 1 (10.5 ounce) can condensed French onion soup
- 1 (10.5 ounce) can beef broth

- 1 (4 ounce) can sliced mushrooms, drained
- 1/4 cup butter

DIRECTIONS

1. Preheat oven to 350 degrees F (175 degrees C).
2. Combine rice, onion soup, beef broth, mushrooms and butter in an 8x8 inch casserole dish.
3. Cover, and bake in the preheated oven for 60 minutes.

INDIAN STYLE BASMATI RICE

Servings: 6 | Prep: 10m | Cooks: 25m | Total: 45m | Additional: 10m

NUTRITION FACTS

Calories: 216.4 | Carbohydrates: 38.9g | Protein: 3.9g | Cholesterol: 0mg | Sodium: 393.7mg

INGREDIENTS

- 1 1/2 cups basmati rice
- 2 tablespoons vegetable oil
- 1 (2 inch) piece cinnamon stick
- 2 pods green cardamom
- 2 eaches whole cloves
- 1 tablespoon cumin seed
- 1 teaspoon salt, or to taste
- 2 1/2 cups water
- 1 small onion, thinly sliced

DIRECTIONS

1. Place rice into a bowl with enough water to cover. Set aside to soak for 20 minutes.
2. Heat the oil in a large pot or saucepan over medium heat. Add the cinnamon stick, cardamom pods, cloves, and cumin seed. Cook and stir for about a minute, then add the onion to the pot. Saute the onion until a rich golden brown, about 10 minutes. Drain the water from the rice, and stir into the pot. Cook and stir the rice for a few minutes, until lightly toasted. Add salt and water to the pot, and bring to a boil. Cover, and reduce heat to low. Simmer for about 15 minutes, or until all of the water has been absorbed. Let stand for 5 minutes, then fluff with a fork before serving.

MEXICAN SOUR CREAM RICE

Servings: 6 | Prep: 20m | Cooks: 30m | Total: 50m

NUTRITION FACTS

Calories: 287.3 | Carbohydrates: 36.9g | Protein: 9.9g | Cholesterol: 34.1mg | Sodium: 772.7mg

INGREDIENTS

- 1 cup uncooked long grain white rice
- 1 (14 ounce) can chicken broth
- 1 cup reduced fat sour cream
- 1 cup shredded Monterey Jack cheese, divided
- 1 (8.75 ounce) can whole kernel corn, drained
- 1/4 cup finely chopped fresh cilantro

- 1 (4 ounce) can diced green chile peppers
- 1 pinch salt and ground black pepper to taste

DIRECTIONS

1. In a large pot, bring the rice and chicken broth to a boil. Reduce heat to low, cover, and simmer 20 minutes.
2. Preheat oven to 350 degrees F (175 degrees C). Lightly grease a 1-1/2 quart casserole dish.
3. In the pot with the cooked rice, mix the sour cream, green chile peppers, 1/2 cup Monterey Jack cheese, corn, and cilantro. Season with salt and pepper. Transfer to the prepared casserole dish, and top with remaining cheese.
4. Bake uncovered 30 minutes in the preheated oven, until cheese is bubbly and lightly browned.

MARIA'S MEXICAN RICE

Servings: 6 | Prep: 10m | Cooks: 30m | Total: 40m

NUTRITION FACTS

Calories: 163.9 | Carbohydrates: 26.8g | Protein: 2.7g | Cholesterol: 0.1mg | Sodium: 845.4mg

INGREDIENTS

- 2 tablespoons olive oil
- 1/8 teaspoon ground black pepper
- 1 cup rice
- 2 1/2 cups water
- 1/2 large onion, diced
- 1/3 cup tomato sauce
- 1/2 tablespoon salt
- 1 tablespoon chicken bouillon (such as Knorr)
- 1/8 teaspoon ground cumin
- 1 whole serrano chile pepper

DIRECTIONS

1. Heat oil in a saucepan over medium heat. Cook and stir rice and onion in the hot oil until browned, about 5 minutes; season with salt, cumin, and pepper. Pour water over the rice mixture. Stir tomato sauce and chicken bouillon into the water. Increase heat to medium-high, place a cover on the saucepan, and bring to a boil. Add serrano chile pepper and continue cooking at a boil for 10 minutes. Reduce heat to medium-low until the rice is tender and the water is absorbed, 15 to 20 minutes more.

SPANISH RICE ORIGINAL

Servings: 6 | Prep: 20m | Cooks: 55m | Total: 1h15m

NUTRITION FACTS

Calories: 372.7 | Carbohydrates: 45.7g | Protein: 8.7g | Cholesterol: 19mg | Sodium: 1195.5mg

INGREDIENTS

- 1 cup chicken broth
- 1 cup tomato sauce
- 6 slices bacon
- 2 onions, diced
- 1 cup uncooked white rice
- 2 tomatoes, diced
- 2 green bell peppers, diced
- 1/2 teaspoon chili powder
- 1/2 teaspoon salt and ground black pepper
- 1 (10 ounce) can sliced black olives, drained
- 1 (10 ounce) can whole kernel corn, drained

DIRECTIONS

1. Bring chicken broth and tomato sauce to a boil in a small saucepan, about 5 minutes. Reduce heat to medium and maintain a simmer while preparing the remaining ingredients.
2. Meanwhile, place bacon in a large skillet and cook over medium-high heat, turning occasionally, until evenly browned, about 10 minutes. Transfer bacon to a paper towel-lined plate, reserving bacon grease in the skillet. Chop bacon.
3. Cook and stir onion in reserved bacon grease over medium heat until tender, about 5 minutes. Stir in rice; cook and stir until lightly browned, 3 to 5 minutes. Pour boiling chicken broth and tomato sauce into rice mixture; add diced tomatoes, green peppers, and chopped bacon. Season with chili powder, salt, and pepper. Cover and simmer until rice is tender and liquid is absorbed, 30 to 40 minutes. Stir black olives and corn into rice mixture before serving.

SPINACH AND RICE (SPANAKORIZO)

Servings: 4 | Prep: 5m | Cooks: 45m | Total: 50m

NUTRITION FACTS

Calories: 336.8 | Carbohydrates: 35.7g | Fat: g | Protein: 9.8g | Cholesterol: 0mg | Sodium: 552.7mg

INGREDIENTS

- 1/3 cup olive oil
- 2 onions, chopped
- 2 pounds fresh spinach, rinsed and stemmed
- 1 (8 ounce) can tomato sauce
- 2 cups water
- 1 teaspoon dried dill weed
- 1 teaspoon dried parsley
- 1/8 teaspoon salt and pepper to taste
- 1/2 cup uncooked white rice

DIRECTIONS

1. Heat olive oil in a large skillet over medium-high heat. Saute onions in the oil until soft and translucent. Add spinach, and cook stirring for a few minutes, then pour in the tomato sauce and water. Bring to a boil, and season with parsley, dill, salt and pepper. Stir in rice, reduce heat to low, and simmer uncovered for 20 to 25 minutes, or until rice is tender. Add more water if necessary.

MARIA'S RICE

Servings: 6 | Prep: 5m | Cooks: 1h | Total: 1h5m

NUTRITION FACTS

Calories: 286 | Carbohydrates: 30.4g | Protein: 4.4g | Cholesterol: 42.6mg | Sodium: 699.7mg

INGREDIENTS

- 1 cup uncooked white rice
- 1 (10.5 ounce) can beef broth
- 1 (10.5 ounce) can condensed French onion soup
- 1/2 cup butter, sliced

DIRECTIONS

1. Preheat oven to 425 degrees F (220 degrees C).
2. In a 9x9 inch baking dish combine rice, soup and broth. Place butter slices on top of the mixture.
3. Cover with foil and bake for 30 minutes. Remove cover and bake 30 minutes more.

MEXICAN RICE

Servings: 8 | Prep: 20m | Cooks: 30m | Total: 50m

NUTRITION FACTS

Calories: 199 | Carbohydrates: 33.8g | Protein: 3.4g | Cholesterol: 0mg | Sodium: 809.4mg

INGREDIENTS

- 3 tablespoons vegetable oil
- 2/3 cup diced onion
- 1 1/2 cups uncooked white rice
- 1 cup chopped green bell pepper
- 1 teaspoon ground cumin
- 1 teaspoon chili powder
- 1 1/2 (8 ounce) cans tomato sauce
- 2 teaspoons salt
- 1 clove garlic, minced
- 1/8 teaspoon powdered saffron
- 3 cups water

DIRECTIONS

1. In a large saucepan, heat vegetable oil over a medium-low heat. Place the onions in the pan, and saute until golden.
2. Add rice to pan, and stir to coat grains with oil. Mix in green bell pepper, cumin, chili powder, tomato sauce, salt, garlic, saffron, and water. Cover, bring to a boil, and then reduce heat to simmer. Cook for 30 to 40 minutes, or until rice is tender. Stir occasionally.

ORZO AND RICE

Servings: 5 | Prep: 5m | Cooks: 25m | Total: 30m

NUTRITION FACTS

Calories: 191.6 | Carbohydrates: 31.7g | Protein: 4.6g | Cholesterol: 12.3mg | Sodium: 265.1mg

Sodium: 265.1mg

INGREDIENTS

- 2 tablespoons butter
- 1/2 cup uncooked orzo pasta
- 1 cube chicken bouillon
- 2 cups water

- 1/2 cup long-grain white
  rice

DIRECTIONS

1. In a large heavy saucepan, melt butter over medium heat; add orzo and brown until golden.
2. Add rice, bouillon, and water; bring to a boil, cover and lower heat to medium-low.
3. Simmer for about 20 to 25 minutes or until all water is absorbed; serve.

BLACK BEANS, CORN, AND YELLOW RICE

Servings: 8 | Prep: 5m | Cooks: 20m | Total: 25m

NUTRITION FACTS

Calories: 99.6 | Carbohydrates: 15.1g | Protein: 2g | Cholesterol: 0mg | Sodium: 195.1mg

INGREDIENTS

- 1 (8 ounce) package yellow rice mix
- 1 1/4 cups water
- 2 tablespoons olive oil
- 1 (15 ounce) can black beans, rinsed and drained
- 1 (15.25 ounce) can whole kernel corn, drained
- 2 teaspoons lime juice
- 1 teaspoon ground cumin

DIRECTIONS

1. Bring the rice, water, and olive oil to a boil in a saucepan over high heat. Reduce heat to medium-low, cover, and simmer until the rice is tender, and the liquid has been absorbed, 20 to 25 minutes.
2. Mix together the beans, corn, lime juice, and cumin in a large bowl. Stir in the cooked rice and serve.

ANN'S DIRTY RICE

Servings: 4 | Prep: 10m | Cooks: 30m | Total: 40m

NUTRITION FACTS

Calories: 438.8 | Carbohydrates: 43.3g | Protein: 23.1g | Cholesterol: 69.8mg | Sodium: 701mg

INGREDIENTS

- 1 pound ground beef
- 1 yellow onion, chopped
- 1 green bell pepper, chopped
- 1 red bell pepper, chopped
- 2 teaspoons beef bouillon granules
- 1/2 teaspoon salt
- 1/2 teaspoon seasoned salt
- 1/2 teaspoon ground black pepper
- 2 cups water
- 1 cup uncooked white rice

DIRECTIONS

1. Heat a large skillet over medium-high heat and stir in the ground beef, onion, green and red peppers, beef bullion, salt, seasoned salt, and pepper. Cook and stir until the beef is crumbly, evenly browned, and no longer pink. Drain and discard any excess grease. Stir in the water and rice. Bring to a boil over high heat, then reduce heat to medium-low, cover, and simmer until the rice is tender, and the liquid has been absorbed, 20 to 25 minutes.

MOM'S SUSHI RICE

Servings: 10 | Prep: 10m | Cooks: 20m | Total: 1h5m | Additional: 35m

NUTRITION FACTS

Calories: 180.7 | Carbohydrates: 40.7g | Protein: 2.9g | Cholesterol: 0mg | Sodium: 296.2mg

INGREDIENTS

- 2 1/4 cups Japanese sushi-style rice
- 1 (4 inch) piece konbu dried kelp
- 3 cups water
- 1/4 cup rice vinegar
- 1/4 cup white sugar
- 1 1/4 teaspoons salt

DIRECTIONS

1. Place rice into a large, deep bowl. Fill with cold water and rub rice together with hands until the water turns milky white. Pour off the cloudy water, being careful not to pour out the rice. Repeat 3 or 4 times until you can see the rice through 3 inches of water.
2. Drain the rice in a fine strainer, then place into a saucepan along with konbu and 3 cups water. Allow to stand for 30 minutes. Stir together rice vinegar, sugar, and salt until dissolved in a small bowl, set aside.

3. Cover, and bring rice to a boil over high heat, then reduce heat to low, and simmer for 15 minutes. Remove from heat and allow to stand, covered, for 5 minutes.
4. Scrape rice into a bowl; remove and discard the konbu. Stir in vinegar mixture until well incorporated and no lumps of rice remain. Allow to cool at room temperature. For a shinier appearance, use an electric fan to cool the rice rapidly.

MEXICAN RICE

Servings: 7 | Prep: 15m | Cooks: 30m | Total: 45m

NUTRITION FACTS

Calories: | Carbohydrates: g | Fat: g | Protein: g | Cholesterol: mg

INGREDIENTS

- 1 1/2 teaspoons vegetable oil
- 1/2 small small onion, diced
- 2/3 cup uncooked long-grain rice
- 1/2 teaspoon ground cumin
- 1/2 teaspoon chili powder
- 3 ounces canned diced tomatoes
- 1 teaspoon salt
- 1 1/2 cups water

DIRECTIONS

1. In a large saucepan, heat oil over medium heat. Stir in onion and saute until translucent.

BROWN RICE

Servings: 4 | Prep: 5m | Cooks: 1h | Total: 1h5m

NUTRITION FACTS

Calories: 425.3 | Carbohydrates: 66.2g | Protein: 8.8g | Cholesterol: 33.4mg | Sodium: 1091mg

INGREDIENTS

- 1 1/2 cups uncooked long-grain white rice
- 1 (14 ounce) can beef broth
- 1 (10.5 ounce) can condensed French onion soup
- 1/4 cup butter, melted
- 1 tablespoon Worcestershire sauce
- 1 tablespoon dried basil leaves

DIRECTIONS

1. Preheat oven to 350 degrees F (175 degrees C).
2. In a 2 quart casserole dish combine rice, broth, soup, butter, Worcestershire sauce and basil.
3. Bake covered for 1 hour, stirring once after 30 minutes.

BAKED MUSHROOM RICE

Servings: 6 | Prep: 15m | Cooks: 40m | Total: 55m

NUTRITION FACTS

Calories: 363.5 | Carbohydrates: 57.9g | Protein: 6.3g | Cholesterol: 20.3mg | Sodium: 461.9mg

INGREDIENTS

- 2 cups uncooked white rice
- 1 (10.75 ounce) can condensed cream of mushroom soup
- 1 cup vegetable broth
- 1/2 cup chopped onion
- 1/4 cup fresh chopped mushrooms
- 1 teaspoon dried parsley
- 1 teaspoon dried oregano
- 1/2 cup butter, melted
- salt and pepper to taste

DIRECTIONS

1. Preheat oven to 400 degrees F (200 degrees C).
2. In a large bowl, stir together the white rice, cream of mushroom soup, and vegetable broth. Blend in the onion, mushrooms, parsley, oregano, melted butter, salt, and pepper. Transfer to a 2 quart baking dish, and cover with a lid or aluminum foil.
3. Bake for 35 to 40 minutes in the preheated oven. If the rice is looking dry before it is tender, then pour in a little water and continue cooking until rice is tender.

PECAN RICE

Servings: 4 | Prep: 5m | Cooks: 40m | Total: 45m

NUTRITION FACTS

Calories: 279.8 | Carbohydrates: 31g | Protein: 4.3g | Cholesterol: 0mg | Sodium: 210mg

INGREDIENTS

- 1 cup brown rice
- 2 tablespoons margarine
- 1/4 cup finely chopped onion
- 1/2 cup finely chopped pecans
- 2 tablespoons minced parsley
- 1/4 teaspoon dried basil
- 1/4 teaspoon ground ginger
- 1/4 teaspoon ground black pepper
- 1/4 teaspoon salt

DIRECTIONS

1. In a saucepan bring 2 cups water to a boil. Add rice and stir. Reduce heat to low, cover and simmer for 40 minutes.
2. When rice is done, melt margarine in a small skillet over medium heat. Saute onions, pecans, parsley, basil, ginger, pepper and salt. When onions are tender stir mixture into rice and mix well.

COCONUT LIME RICE

Servings: 2 | Prep: 5m | Cooks: 30m | Total: 40m | Additional: 5m

NUTRITION FACTS

Calories: 684.6 | Carbohydrates: 85.4g | Protein: 10g | Cholesterol: 5.4mg | Sodium: 56.3mg

INGREDIENTS

- 1 cup basmati rice
- 1 tablespoon coconut oil
- 1 teaspoon butter
- 1/4 cup flaked coconut
- 1 cup coconut milk
- 1 cup chicken broth
- 1 pinch salt, to taste
- 1 lime, zested and juiced
- 1 pinch ground black pepper, to taste

DIRECTIONS

1. Rinse rice until the water runs clear; drain. Heat coconut oil and butter in a large skillet over medium-high heat. Cook and stir rice and coconut flakes for 3 to 4 minutes. Stir in the lime juice, then add the coconut milk, chicken broth, salt and lime zest. Bring to a low boil, then cover and reduce heat to low. Cook for 20 minutes. Remove from heat and keep covered for 5 minutes. Fluff with fork and season with pepper.

COCONUT LIME RICE

Servings: 2 | Prep: 5m | Cooks: 30m | Total: 40m | Additional: 5m

NUTRITION FACTS

Calories: 684.6 | Carbohydrates: 85.4g | Protein: 10g | Cholesterol: 5.4mg | Sodium: 56.3mg

INGREDIENTS

- 1 cup basmati rice
- 1 tablespoon coconut oil
- 1 teaspoon butter
- 1/4 cup flaked coconut
- 1 cup coconut milk
- 1 cup chicken broth
- 1 pinch salt, to taste
- 1 lime, zested and juiced
- 1 pinch ground black pepper, to taste

DIRECTIONS

1. Rinse rice until the water runs clear; drain. Heat coconut oil and butter in a large skillet over medium-high heat. Cook and stir rice and coconut flakes for 3 to 4 minutes. Stir in the lime juice, then add the coconut milk, chicken broth, salt and lime zest. Bring to a low boil, then cover and reduce heat to low. Cook for 20 minutes. Remove from heat and keep covered for 5 minutes. Fluff with fork and season with pepper.

HAZELNUT-MUSHROOM PILAF

Servings: 6 | Prep: 10m | Cooks: 30m | Total: 40m

NUTRITION FACTS

Calories: 256 | Carbohydrates: 23.9g | Fat: 14.7g | Protein: 8.1g | Cholesterol: 21mg | Sodium: 584mg

INGREDIENTS

- 1/4 cup butter
- 1/2 cup uncooked long-grain rice
- 1/4 cup uncooked orzo pasta
- 1/2 cup sliced fresh mushrooms
- 2 cups chicken broth
- 2 tablespoons chopped fresh parsley
- 1/4 teaspoon dried marjoram
- 1/4 teaspoon ground black pepper

- 1/2 cup chopped onion
- 1/4 cup minced celery
- 1/2 cup chopped toasted hazelnuts

DIRECTIONS

1. Place a large skillet over medium-low heat. Melt butter, then saute rice, orzo, mushrooms, onion, and celery. Stir constantly until rice is lightly browned.
2. Mix in chicken broth, parsley, marjoram, pepper, and hazelnuts. Bring to a boil, then reduce heat to low, cover skillet, and allow to simmer 15 minutes. Remove from heat and let stand 10 minutes before serving.

BAKED MUSHROOM RISOTTO

Servings: 4 | Prep: 10m | Cooks: 35m | Total: 45m

NUTRITION FACTS

Calories: 480 | Carbohydrates: 51.1g | Fat: 25.9g | Protein: 11.1g | Cholesterol: 86mg | Sodium: 998mg

INGREDIENTS

- 3 tablespoons butter
- 3 cups diced mushrooms
- salt to taste
- 1/2 yellow onion, diced
- ground black pepper to taste
- 1 pinch cayenne pepper
- 1 cup carnaroli rice
- 2 cups chicken broth, divided
- 1/2 cup heavy whipping cream
- 1/2 cup chicken broth
- 2 tablespoons heavy whipping cream
- 1/2 cup finely grated Parmigiano-Reggiano cheese
- 2 tablespoons chopped fresh chives

DIRECTIONS

1. Preheat oven to 400 degrees F (200 degrees C).
2. Melt butter in large, oven-proof skillet over medium-high heat. Add mushrooms; season with salt, and cook and stir mushrooms until brown. They will begin browning after the moisture evaporates.
3. Reduce heat to medium and stir in onion. Sprinkle with black pepper and cayenne pepper. Cook and stir until onions are translucent and soft.
4. Pour rice into skillet and stir until each rice grain is coated with butter. Season with salt.

5. Pour 1 cup chicken broth into the rice mixture. Raise heat to medium-high and cook, stirring rice until liquid is completely absorbed by the rice.
6. Pour another cup chicken stock into the rice and stir until mixture comes to a simmer.
7. Bake in preheated oven until grains are almost tender but still slightly firm, about 15 minutes. Transfer skillet to stovetop. Season with more salt, if necessary.
8. Combine the remaining 1/2 cup chicken broth and cream; pour into the skillet. Cook on medium heat, stirring constantly until rice is tender, 1 or 2 minutes. Remove skillet from heat.
9. Drizzle 2 tablespoons cream over rice. Add the grated Parmigiano-Reggiano and chives; stir. Serve immediately.

BROCCOLI AND RICE STIR FRY

Servings: 8 | Prep: 5m | Cooks: 25m | Total: 30m

NUTRITION FACTS

Calories: 187 | Carbohydrates: 32.9g | Protein: 6.3g | Cholesterol: 46.5mg | Sodium: 403.9mg

INGREDIENTS

- 1 1/2 cups uncooked long-grain rice
- 1 tablespoon vegetable oil
- 1 (16 ounce) package frozen broccoli florets, thawed
- 3 green onions, diced
- 2 eggs, beaten
- 2 tablespoons soy sauce
- 1/2 teaspoon salt
- 1/4 teaspoon ground black pepper

DIRECTIONS

1. In a saucepan, bring 3 cups water to a boil. Stir in rice. Reduce heat, cover, and simmer for 20 minutes.
2. Heat oil in a large skillet over medium heat. Saute broccoli until tender crisp, and add scallions. Remove from skillet. Scramble eggs; return broccoli mixture to pan. Stir in cooked rice, soy sauce, salt and pepper.

CAJUN DIRTY RICE

Servings: 8 | Prep: 15m | Cooks: 35m | Total: 50m

NUTRITION FACTS

Calories: 484.8 | Carbohydrates: 41.4g | Protein: 26.2g | Cholesterol: 72.3mg | Sodium: 1541.4mg

INGREDIENTS

- 1 pound lean ground beef
- 1 pound beef sausage
- 1 onion, finely diced
- 1 (8 ounce) package dirty rice mix
- 2 cups water
- 1 (10 ounce) can diced tomatoes with green chile peppers
- 2 (15 ounce) cans kidney beans, drained
- salt and pepper to taste

DIRECTIONS

1. In a skillet over medium heat, brown the ground beef, sausage, and onion; drain.
2. In a large pan, combine rice mix and 2 cups water. Add diced tomatoes and chilies. Stir in the kidney beans. Bring to a boil, then add meat mixture. Season with salt and pepper. Return to boil, reduce heat, and cover, stirring occasionally. Cook for 25 minutes, until rice is easily fluffed with a fork.

AUTHENTIC NEW ORLEANS RED BEANS AND RICE

Servings: 10 | Prep: 20m | Cooks: 5h10m | Total: 5h30m

NUTRITION FACTS

Calories: 465.1 | Carbohydrates: 44.1g | Protein: 25.9g | Cholesterol: 44.5mg | Sodium: 861.3mg

INGREDIENTS

- 1 tablespoon shortening, or as needed
- 1 white onion, chopped
- 3 cloves garlic, chopped
- 1 green bell pepper, chopped
- 8 cups water
- 1 pound dried red beans
- 1 smoked ham hock
- 1 pound smoked sausage, cut into bite-sized pieces
- 2 stalks celery, chopped
- 2 eaches bay leaves
- 1 tablespoon Creole seasoning (such as Tony Chachere's)
- 1/2 teaspoon dried thyme
- 1/2 teaspoon dried sage
- 1 dash hot pepper sauce (such as Tabasco®), or to taste
- 3 cups cooked white rice

DIRECTIONS

1. Melt shortening in a skillet over medium heat. Cook and stir onion, garlic, and bell pepper in hot shortening until tender, 5 to 7 minutes.
2. Combine water, red beans, and ham hock in a large pot; bring to a boil. Stir onion mixture into the water; add smoked sausage and celery to the boiling water; return to a boil. Stir bay leaves, Creole seasoning, thyme, and sage into the boiling water. Reduce heat to low, place a cover on the pot, and simmer until the beans are tender, about 5 hours.
3. Remove and discard ham hock and bay leaves; stir in hot pepper sauce and serve over white rice.

LINNIE'S SPANISH RICE

Servings: 4 | Prep: 10m | Cooks: 30m | Total: 40m

NUTRITION FACTS

Calories: 200.1 | Carbohydrates: 44.2g | Protein: 5.1g | Cholesterol: 0mg | Sodium: 674.4mg

INGREDIENTS

- 1 cup uncooked white rice
- 2 cups water
- 1 teaspoon minced garlic
- 1 (16 ounce) jar salsa

DIRECTIONS

1. Combine the rice with the garlic in a large saucepan. Pour water and salsa into the rice mixture. Bring the water to a full boil and then reduce the temperature to simmer. Simmer for 20 minutes or until the rice is tender. Fluff the rice when finished.

SPANISH RICE

Servings: 6 | Prep: 20m | Cooks: 40m | Total: 1h

NUTRITION FACTS

Calories: 268.7 | Carbohydrates: 54.8g | Protein: 5.2g | Cholesterol: 0mg | Sodium: 153.4mg

INGREDIENTS

- 1 tablespoon vegetable oil
- 2 cups uncooked long-grain white rice
- 1/4 onion, chopped
- salt and pepper to taste
- 1 (14.5 ounce) can stewed tomatoes
- 4 cups water

- 1 green bell pepper,
  chopped

DIRECTIONS

1. In a large skillet, combine oil, rice, onion, green pepper and salt and pepper until the rice is a light brown color. Remove skillet from stove.
2. Mix tomatoes into the mixture. Pour in water (it should cover the entire mixture; use more if necessary). Return the skillet to the stovetop and bring the mixture to a full boil; salt and pepper to taste. When the mixture begins to boil, cover the skillet, and reduce heat to a simmer. Cook 12 to 15 minutes and never, I mean NEVER, remove the cover. After 12 to 15 minutes, turn stove off and let stand for another 12 to 15 minutes. DO NOT remove cover until the final 15 minutes has elapsed!

INDIAN SAFFRON RICE

Servings: 6 | Prep: 5m | Cooks: 20m | Total: 25m

NUTRITION FACTS

Calories: 154.2 | Carbohydrates: 26.1g | Protein: 2.5g | Cholesterol: 10.2mg | Sodium: 418.2mg

INGREDIENTS

- 1/8 teaspoon powdered saffron
- 2 cups boiling water, divided
- 2 tablespoons butter
- 1 cup uncooked long-grain white rice, not rinsed
- 1 teaspoon salt

DIRECTIONS

1. Steep the saffron in 1/2 cup boiling water.
2. In a skillet that can be tightly covered, melt the butter over medium-high heat. Stir in the rice and salt. Cook, stirring constantly, until the rice begins to absorb the butter and becomes opaque, but do not brown the rice.
3. Quickly pour in the remaining 1 1/2 cups boiling water along with the saffron water. Cover immediately, reduce heat to low, and cook 20 minutes, or until all of the liquid is absorbed. For best results, do not remove the lid while the rice is cooking.

LEMON BASMATI RICE

Servings: 4 | Prep: 10m | Cooks: 20m | Total: 30m

NUTRITION FACTS

Calories: 194 | Carbohydrates: 40.3g | Fat: 3g | Protein: 3.9g | Cholesterol: 0mg | Sodium: 1mg

INGREDIENTS

- 2 teaspoons canola oil
- 1 cup basmati rice, rinsed
- 1 (2 inch) piece fresh ginger, minced
- 1 lemon, juiced and zested
- 2 cups chicken broth
- salt and ground black pepper to taste

DIRECTIONS

1. Heat the oil in a pot over medium heat. Cook the rice, ginger, and lemon zest together in the hot oil for about 1 minute; add the lemon juice and chicken broth. Bring the mixture to a boil; cover the pot and allow the mixture to simmer until the liquid is absorbed and the rice is tender, 18 to 20 minutes. Season with salt and pepper.

SOUTHERN DIRTY RICE

Servings: 8 | Prep: 15m | Cooks: 30m | Total: 45m

NUTRITION FACTS

Calories: 251.6 | Carbohydrates: 41.7g | Protein: 11.5g | Cholesterol: 127.4mg | Sodium: 28.8mg

INGREDIENTS

- 1/4 pound chicken gizzards, rinsed
- 1/2 pound chicken livers, rinsed and trimmed
- 1 tablespoon vegetable oil
- 1 onion, finely chopped
- 3 cloves garlic, minced
- 2 cups uncooked white rice
- 4 cups chicken broth
- 1 pinch salt to taste
- 1/2 teaspoon ground black pepper
- 1/4 teaspoon cayenne pepper
- 1 cup thinly sliced green onions

DIRECTIONS

1. Pulse gizzards in food processor, then pulse livers.
2. Heat oil in a large saucepan. Saute onion and gizzards over medium heat, stirring constantly, until meat begins to brown (about 5 minutes). Add livers and garlic and cook, stirring constantly, until brown (about 3 minutes).
3. Add rice and stir until coated with oil. Add broth, salt, pepper and cayenne pepper. Bring to a boil, then reduce heat to simmer. Cover and cook about 20 minutes, until rice has absorbed liquid. Sprinkle with green onion and serve.

RICE WITH HERBES DE PROVENCE

Servings: 4 | Prep: 2m | Cooks: 23m | Total: 25m

NUTRITION FACTS

Calories: 169.4 | Carbohydrates: 37.1g | Protein: 3.3g | Cholesterol: 0mg | Sodium: 82.4mg

INGREDIENTS

- 1 cup white rice
- 2 cups chicken stock
- 11/2 teaspoons herbes de Provence
- 1 pinch sea salt
- 1 pinch pepper

DIRECTIONS

1. In a medium saucepan stir together rice, chicken stock, herbes de Provence, salt, and pepper. Set over high heat, and bring to a simmer; cover, and cook 20 minutes. Fluff with a fork, and serve.

VEGAN CURRIED RICE

Servings: 4 | Prep: 5m | Cooks: 25m | Total: 30m

NUTRITION FACTS

Calories: 262.4 | Carbohydrates: 42.8g | Protein: 4.8g | Cholesterol: 0mg | Sodium: 253.2mg

INGREDIENTS

- 2 tablespoons olive oil
- 1 tablespoon minced garlic
- 1 tablespoon chili powder, or to taste
- 1 cube vegetable bouillon

- black pepper to taste

- 1 tablespoon ground cumin, or to taste

- 1 tablespoon ground curry powder, or to taste

- 1 cup water

- 1 tablespoon soy sauce

- 1 cup uncooked white rice

DIRECTIONS

1. Heat olive oil in a medium saucepan over low heat. Sweat the garlic; when the garlic becomes aromatic, slowly stir in pepper, cumin, curry powder and chili powder. When spices begin to fry and become fragrant, stir in the bouillon cube and a little water.
2. Increase heat to high and add the rest of the water and the soy sauce. Just before the mixture comes to a boil, stir in rice. Bring to a rolling boil; reduce heat to low, cover, and simmer 15 to 20 minutes, or until all liquid is absorbed.
3. Remove from heat and let stand 5 minutes.

ITALIAN RICE BALLS

Servings: 8 | Prep: 45m | Cooks: 15m | Total: 2h | Additional: 1h

NUTRITION FACTS

Calories: 683.4 | Carbohydrates: 34.7g | Protein: 7.3g | Cholesterol: 37.6mg | Sodium: 804.8mg

INGREDIENTS

- 2 eggs

- 1/3 cup grated Parmesan cheese

- 1 tablespoon dried parsley

- 1/4 teaspoon freshly ground black pepper

- 1 teaspoon salt

- 1 quart water

- 1 teaspoon salt

- 1 cup uncooked white rice

- 1 1/2 cups dried bread crumbs

- 2 cups olive oil

DIRECTIONS

1. In a medium bowl, whisk together eggs, cheese, parsley, pepper, and 1 teaspoon salt. Cover and refrigerate.
2. Pour water and 1 teaspoon salt into a large saucepan and bring to a boil. Stir in rice and reduce heat to low. Cook rice until water is almost absorbed, stirring frequently. Remove from heat and slowly

pour in egg mixture, stirring rapidly to prevent egg from scrambling. Allow rice mixture to cool for 1 hour.

3. Pour bread crumbs into a pile on one end of a cutting board. Dampen hands and roll rice mixture into 1 inch balls, then coat each one with bread crumbs.
4. In a small, deep skillet, heat olive oil to 350 degrees F (175 degrees C). (Should have enough oil to completely cover rice balls.) Fry rice balls 6 at a time, turning as needed to ensure even browning. Drain on paper towels and serve warm.

TACO RICE

Servings: 4 | Prep: 5m | Cooks: 10m | Total: 15m

NUTRITION FACTS

Calories: 458.8 | Carbohydrates: 42.6g | Protein: 12.7g | Cholesterol: 55mg | Sodium: 139.8mg

INGREDIENTS

- 1 (14.5 ounce) can chicken broth
- 1 (8 ounce) can tomato sauce
- 1 (1 ounce) package taco seasoning mix
- 1 1/2 cups uncooked instant rice
- 1 (6 ounce) can black olives, drained and chopped
- 1 cup shredded Cheddar cheese
- 1 cup sour cream

DIRECTIONS

1. In a large pot, bring chicken broth, tomato sauce, and taco seasoning to a boil.
2. Stir rice into the pot, cover and remove from heat. Let the pot stand, covered, for 5 minutes.
3. Stir in cheese and olives; mix well. Serve with sour cream.

CASHEW RAISIN RICE PILAF

Servings: 12 | Prep: 15m | Cooks: 30m | Total: 45m

NUTRITION FACTS

Calories: 270.2 | Carbohydrates: 41.3g | Protein: 6.5g | Cholesterol: 0mg | Sodium: 346.4mg

INGREDIENTS

- 1/4 cup margarine
- 3/4 cup uncooked wild rice

- 1 1/2 cups uncooked long grain white rice
- 1 chopped onion
- 1 cup chopped carrot
- 1 cup golden raisins
- 3 cups chicken broth
- 2 cups frozen green peas
- 1 (4 ounce) jar diced pimento peppers, drained
- 1 cup cashews
- 1 teaspoon salt
- ground black pepper to taste

DIRECTIONS

1. Melt margarine in a large saucepan over medium-high heat. Saute the long grain rice, onion, carrot and raisins for 3 to 5 minutes or until onion is tender. Pour in the broth and bring to a boil. Reduce heat to low, cover pan and simmer for 20 to 25 minutes.
2. Meanwhile, in a saucepan bring 1 1/2 cups salted water to a boil. Add wild rice, reduce heat, cover and simmer for 45 minutes. Drain and set aside.
3. When the rice/raisin mixture is finished simmering (rice is cooked), stir in cooked wild rice, peas, pimentos and cashews and heat through.

EASY AUTHENTIC MEXICAN RICE

Servings: 8 | Prep: 5m | Cooks: 20m | Total: 25m

NUTRITION FACTS

Calories: 158.1 | Carbohydrates: 21.1g | Protein: 2.2g | Cholesterol: 0mg | Sodium: 124.1mg

INGREDIENTS

- 1/4 cup canola oil
- 1 tablespoon onion powder
- 1 tablespoon garlic powder
- 1 cup uncooked white rice
- 1 1/2 cups water
- 1 (6.5 ounce) can tomato sauce

DIRECTIONS

1. Heat canola oil in a skillet over medium-high heat. Season oil with onion powder and garlic powder. Cook and stir rice in seasoned oil until rice is golden, 2 to 4 minutes.
2. Pour water and tomato sauce over the rice; stir. Bring the mixture to a boil, cover the skillet, reduce heat to medium-low, and simmer until the rice is tender, about 15 minutes.

JASMINE RICE

Servings: 4 | Prep: 10m | Cooks: 50m | Total: 1h

NUTRITION FACTS

Calories: 325.1 | Carbohydrates: 59.1g | Protein: 5.3g | Cholesterol: 0mg | Sodium: 0.8mg

INGREDIENTS

- 2 tablespoons olive oil
- 2 tablespoons chopped onion
- 1/4 cup green peas
- 1 bay leaf
- 1 1/2 cups dry jasmine rice
- 3 cups water
- salt to taste

DIRECTIONS

1. In a large saucepan over a medium-low heat, warm the oil. Add onion and saute for 3 to 5 minutes. Mix in green peas, bay leaf, and jasmine rice. Stir to coat the rice.
2. Pour 3 cups water into the saucepan and add the salt. Increase the heat to medium and let the rice come to a quick simmer. Reduce heat to low and let rice simmer lightly and sit uncovered until all of the liquid is absorbed. Cover the rice and remove from heat, let sit approximately 40 minutes.

INDIAN-STYLE RICE WITH CASHEWS, RAISINS AND TURMERIC

Servings: 6 | Prep: 5m | Cooks: 22m | Total: 27m

NUTRITION FACTS

Calories: 461.9 | Carbohydrates: 55.8g | Protein: 8.4g | Cholesterol: 2mg | Sodium: 791.7mg

INGREDIENTS

- 1 tablespoon vegetable oil
- 1 1/2 cups basmati rice
- 1 (14 ounce) can coconut milk
- 1 1/4 (14 ounce) cans chicken stock
- 1 pinch crushed red pepper flakes
- 1 teaspoon salt
- 1/4 teaspoon ground turmeric
- 1 bay leaf

- 1/2 teaspoon ground cumin
- 1/2 teaspoon ground coriander
- 1/2 cup raisins
- 3/4 cup cashew halves

DIRECTIONS

1. Heat oil in a large pot over medium-high heat. Stir in rice, and cook for 2 minutes. Pour in the coconut milk, chicken stock, cumin, coriander, red pepper flakes, salt, turmeric, bay leaf, raisins, and cashew halves. Bring to a boil, then cover, and reduce heat to low. Cook until rice is tender, about 20 minutes.

CINDY'S YELLOW RICE

Servings: 4 | Prep: 10m | Cooks: 20m | Total: 30m

NUTRITION FACTS

Calories: 253 | Carbohydrates: 42.8g | Protein: 3.8g | Cholesterol: 0mg | Sodium: 586.9mg

INGREDIENTS

- 2 cups water
- 1 cup white rice
- 1/4 cup dried minced onion
- 2 tablespoons olive oil
- 1 teaspoon ground turmeric
- 1 teaspoon garlic powder
- 1 teaspoon ground black pepper
- 1 teaspoon salt

DIRECTIONS

1. Bring water to a boil in a saucepan. Add rice, onion, olive oil, turmeric, garlic powder, black pepper, and salt. Cover the saucepan, reduce heat to low, and simmer until water is absorbed and rice is cooked, about 20 minutes. Fluff rice with a fork.

DIRTY RICE

Servings: 6 | Prep: 20m | Cooks: 25m | Total: 45m

NUTRITION FACTS

Calories: 409.1 | Carbohydrates: 71.4g | Protein: 13.7g | Cholesterol: 0mg | Sodium: 424.2mg

INGREDIENTS

- 2 tablespoons olive oil
- 3 cloves garlic, minced
- 1 cup chopped onion
- 1 green bell pepper, chopped
- 1 tablespoon chili powder
- 2 teaspoons annatto or achiote powder
- 1/4 teaspoon crushed red pepper
- 1 teaspoon ground cumin
- 1/4 teaspoon ground cinnamon
- 1 1/3 cups uncooked white rice
- 2 3/4 cups water
- 1 teaspoon salt
- 3 roma (plum) tomatoes, chopped
- 1 1/3 cups whole corn kernels, blanched
- 1 cup black beans, cooked and drained
- 1/4 cup toasted pine nuts
- freshly ground black pepper
- 1 red onion, thinly sliced
- 1 tablespoon fresh lime juice
- 2 tablespoons chopped fresh cilantro
- 1 lime, cut into wedges
- 2 teaspoons annatto powder

DIRECTIONS

1. In a heavy saucepan, heat 1 tablespoon of the olive oil over medium heat. Add the garlic and the chopped onions; saute for 5 minutes, stirring frequently. Mix in the bell pepper, chili powder, ground annatto, chili flakes, cumin, and cinnamon. Saute for 2 minutes.
2. Pour the rice into the saucepan and stir to coat. Add the water and 1 teaspoon salt, and bring the rice to a boil over high heat. Cover the pan and turn the heat to low. Simmer the rice for 25 minutes.
3. When the rice is cooked, mix in tomatoes, corn, black beans, and pine nuts. Stir in salt, pepper and lime juice. When the mixture is heated through, spoon it onto plates and top with the sliced red onion and cilantro. Serve a wedge or two of lime with each plate to squeeze over the rice.

ARMENIAN RICE PILAF

Servings: 6 | Prep: 5m | Cooks: 30m | Total: 35m

NUTRITION FACTS

Calories: 535.4 | Carbohydrates: 84.9g | Protein: 9.2g | Cholesterol: 48mg | Sodium: 1976.1mg

INGREDIENTS

- 1/2 cup butter
- 1 1/2 cups uncooked fine egg noodles
- 3 cups uncooked long grain white rice
- 5 (14.5 ounce) cans chicken broth
- 4 cubes chicken bouillon

DIRECTIONS

1. Melt butter in large saucepan over medium-high heat. Add the egg noodles and stir until they begin to brown, being careful not to burn the butter. Stir in the rice. Continue stirring until rice is coated with butter.
2. Pour in the chicken broth and add the bouillon cubes. Bring to a boil; reduce heat to low and cover tightly. Cook without uncovering pot until all the liquid has been absorbed, about 20 minutes.

MY FAVORITE MEXICAN RICE

Servings: 6 | Prep: 10m | Cooks: 40m | Total: 50m

NUTRITION FACTS

Calories: 293.7 | Carbohydrates: 28.4g | Protein: 9.8g | Cholesterol: 25.1mg | Sodium: 1053.1mg

INGREDIENTS

- 3 tablespoons vegetable oil
- 1 cup long grain white rice
- 2 1/2 cups chicken broth
- 1 (4 ounce) can tomato sauce
- 1 (4 ounce) can canned chopped green chiles, drained
- 1 small onion, minced
- 2 cloves garlic, minced
- 1 1/2 teaspoons salt
- 1/2 teaspoon ground cumin
- 1/4 teaspoon chili powder
- 1 1/2 cups shredded Monterey Jack cheese

DIRECTIONS

1. Heat vegetable oil in a large skillet over medium heat. Stir in rice; cook and stir until rice is lightly browned and gives off a toasted fragrance, 5 to 7 minutes. Stir in the chicken broth, tomato sauce, green chiles, onion, garlic, salt, cumin, and chili powder. Bring to a boil, then reduce heat to low.

Cover and simmer until rice is tender, about 25 minutes, stirring occasionally. Spread Monterey Jack cheese on top, then replace the lid and allow the cheese to melt, about 5 minutes more.

EASY PILAF

Servings: 6 | Prep: 10m | Cooks: 40m | Total: 50m

NUTRITION FACTS

Calories: 162.3 | Carbohydrates: 27.9g | Protein: 2.8g | Cholesterol: 10.2mg | Sodium: 416.3mg

INGREDIENTS

- 2 tablespoons butter
- 1 onion, chopped
- 1 cup uncooked white rice
- 2 cups chicken broth
- 1 teaspoon salt

DIRECTIONS

1. Preheat an oven to 375 degrees F (190 degrees C). Prepare a 1 quart baking dish with butter.
2. Melt the butter in a large skillet over medium-high heat. Fry the onion in the butter until translucent, 3 to 5 minutes. Stir in the rice; cook until the rice is slightly golden. Pour in the chicken broth. Season with the salt. Simmer another 5 minutes. Transfer to the prepared dish.
3. Bake in the preheated oven until the broth is completely absorbed, 35 to 40 minutes. Fluff with a fork to serve.

RICE-SO-NICE

Servings: 4 | Prep: 5m | Cooks: 1h | Total: 1h5m

NUTRITION FACTS

Calories: 437 | Carbohydrates: 47g | Protein: 7.1g | Cholesterol: 63.9mg | Sodium: 1170.2mg

INGREDIENTS

- 1 cup long grain white rice
- 1/2 cup butter
- 1 (10.5 ounce) can beef broth
- 1 (10.5 ounce) can condensed French onion soup
- 1 (4 ounce) can sliced mushrooms

DIRECTIONS

1. Preheat the oven to 375 degrees F (190 degrees C).
2. Put the rice in a medium oven-proof bowl. Pour in the beef broth and French onion soup. Empty the can of mushrooms into the bowl, and place the stick of butter in without stirring. Cover the bowl with foil, a lid or oven-proof plate.
3. Bake for 1 hour in the preheated oven. Remove the bowl from the oven and stir. Let stand for a few minutes before serving.

ORANGE CILANTRO RICE

Servings: 6 | Prep: 10m | Cooks: 25m | Total: 35m

NUTRITION FACTS

Calories: 170.9 | Carbohydrates: 34.6g | Protein: 3.4g | Cholesterol: 3.6mg | Sodium: 208.6mg

INGREDIENTS

- 2 teaspoons butter
- 1/2 cup diced onion
- 1 cup uncooked long grain white rice
- 2 teaspoons ground cumin
- 1/2 teaspoon garlic powder
- 1/2 teaspoon onion powder
- 1/4 teaspoon ground black pepper
- 1/8 teaspoon cayenne pepper
- 1/2 teaspoon salt to taste
- 1 1/2 cups orange juice
- 1/2 cup chicken broth
- 1/2 cup chopped fresh cilantro

DIRECTIONS

1. Melt the butter in a saucepan over medium-high heat. Stir in onion, and cook until tender. Mix in rice, and season with cumin, garlic powder, onion powder, pepper, cayenne pepper, and salt. Cook and stir until rice is golden brown. Pour in orange juice and broth, and bring to a boil. Reduce heat to low, cover and simmer 20 minutes.
2. Remove cooked rice from heat, and gently mix in cilantro to serve.

RICE & BEANS (HAITIAN STYLE)

Servings: 6 | Prep: 15m | Cooks: 2h | Total: 2h15m

NUTRITION FACTS

Calories: 341.4 | Carbohydrates: 52.2g | Protein: 11.7g | Cholesterol: 0mg | Sodium: 975.3mg

INGREDIENTS

- 1 (8 ounce) package dry kidney beans
- 4 tablespoons olive oil
- 1 bulb shallot, minced
- 3 cloves garlic, minced
- 1 cup uncooked long grain white rice
- 2 bay leaves
- 1 teaspoon adobo seasoning
- 1 tablespoon kosher salt
- 1/2 teaspoon freshly ground black pepper to taste
- 1/4 teaspoon ground cloves
- 3 sprigs fresh parsley
- 3 sprigs fresh thyme
- 1 scotch bonnet chile pepper

DIRECTIONS

1. Place beans in a large pot, and cover with 3 inches of water. Bring to a boil, reduce heat, and simmer 1 1/2 hours, or until tender. Drain, reserving liquid.
2. Heat oil in a large skillet over medium heat. Saute shallot and garlic until fragrant. Stir in cooked beans, and cook for 2 minutes. Measure reserved liquid, and add water to equal 5 cups; stir into skillet. Stir in the uncooked rice. Season with bay leaves, adobo seasoning, salt, pepper, and cloves. Place sprigs of parsley and thyme, and scotch bonnet pepper on top, and bring to a boil. Reduce heat, cover, and simmer for 18 to 20 minutes. Remove thyme, parsley, and scotch bonnet pepper to serve.

EASY COCONUT RICE

Servings: 8 | Prep: 5m | Cooks: 30m | Total: 35m

NUTRITION FACTS

Calories: 256.4 | Carbohydrates: 39g | Protein: 4.3g | Cholesterol: 0mg | Sodium: 154.4mg

INGREDIENTS

- 2 cups long grain rice, rinsed and drained
- 1/4 cup diced onion
- 1 1/2 cups coconut milk
- 3/4 cup water
- 2 slices fresh ginger root
- 2 teaspoons curry powder
- 1/2 teaspoon salt

DIRECTIONS

1. In a medium saucepan, combine rice, onion, coconut milk, water, ginger, curry powder, and salt. Cover, and bring to a boil. Reduce heat, and simmer for 20 to 30 minutes, or until done.

CINNAMON RICE WITH APPLES

Servings: 4 | Prep: 10m | Cooks: 20m | Total: 30m

NUTRITION FACTS

Calories: 240.1 | Carbohydrates: 56.1g | Protein: 3.5g | Cholesterol: 0mg | Sodium: 153.2mg

INGREDIENTS

- 3/4 cup uncooked white rice
- 1 1/2 cups apple juice
- 1 apple, cored and chopped
- 1/3 cup raisins
- 1/2 teaspoon ground cinnamon
- 1/4 teaspoon salt, or to taste
- 1/4 cup chopped fresh parsley

DIRECTIONS

1. In a saucepan, combine rice, apple juice, chopped apple, and raisins. Season with cinnamon and salt. Bring to a boil, reduce heat to low, and cover for about 17 minutes. Lift lid, and see if rice is moist enough for your taste; if not, cook another couple minutes.
2. Mix in fresh parsley. Serve immediately.

BASMATI RICE

Servings: 4 | Prep: 10m | Cooks: 20m | Total: 30m

NUTRITION FACTS

Calories: 174.5 | Carbohydrates: 38.3g | Protein: 4.1g | Cholesterol: 0mg | Sodium: 0mg

INGREDIENTS

- 1 3/4 cups water
- 1/4 cup frozen green peas
- 1 cup basmati rice
- 1 teaspoon cumin seeds

DIRECTIONS

1. In a saucepan bring water to a boil. Add rice and stir. Reduce heat, cover and simmer for 20 minutes.
2. When rice is cooked, stir in peas and cumin. Cover and let stand for 5 minutes.

ONION RICE PILAF

Servings: 4 | Prep: 5m | Cooks: 40m | Total: 45m

NUTRITION FACTS

Calories: 207.8 | Carbohydrates: 40.3g | Protein: 3.4g | Cholesterol: 7.6mg | Sodium: 21.1mg

INGREDIENTS

- 1/2 small onion, chopped
- 1 tablespoon butter
- 1 cup uncooked calrose rice, rinsed
- 1 1/2 cups chicken broth

DIRECTIONS

1. Heat the butter in a skillet over medium heat. Stir in the onion, and cook until soft and translucent.
2. In a small saucepan, combine the rice, onions, and broth. Bring to a boil over high heat. Reduce heat to low, cover, and simmer 30 minutes. Remove from heat, let cool for several minutes, then fluff with a fork.

CREOLE BLACK-EYED PEAS AND RICE

Servings: 6 | Prep: 10m | Cooks: 45m | Total: 55m

NUTRITION FACTS

Calories: 387.6 | Carbohydrates: 48.7g | Protein: 24.1g | Cholesterol: 49.6mg | Sodium: 720.7mg

INGREDIENTS

- 1 pound lean ground beef
- 2 small onions, chopped
- 1 cup chopped green bell pepper
- 1 cup long grain white rice
- 2 cups water
- 1 tablespoon Creole seasoning
- 1 teaspoon ground black pepper
- 1/2 teaspoon garlic powder
- 2 (15.5 ounce) cans black-eyed peas, drained

DIRECTIONS

1. Crumble the ground beef into a deep skillet or large saucepan over medium-high heat. Add the onions and green pepper. Cook and stir until beef is evenly browned. Drain the grease.
2. Add the rice and water to the pan, and season with Creole seasoning, pepper, and garlic powder. Bring to a boil, then cover and reduce heat to low. Simmer for 30 minutes, until the water is absorbed. About halfway through cooking the rice, stir in the black-eyed peas.

RED BEANS AND RICE WITH SAUSAGE

Servings: 8 | Prep: 10m | Cooks: 3h20m | Total: 11h30m | Additional: 8h

NUTRITION FACTS

Calories: 345.1 | Carbohydrates: 12.2g | Protein: 20.2g | Cholesterol: 55.6mg | Sodium: 1449.8mg

INGREDIENTS

- 2 cups dried red beans
- 1/2 teaspoon dried minced garlic
- 1 tablespoon dried minced onion
- 2 teaspoons salt
- 1/4 teaspoon ground cayenne pepper
- 1 teaspoon celery seed
- 1 teaspoon ground cumin
- 1/4 teaspoon crushed red pepper flakes

- 1 bay leaf

- 1 teaspoon white sugar

- 1 ham hock

- 1 pound smoked sausage, sliced

DIRECTIONS

1. Pick over the dried beans, and soak them in water overnight.
2. The next day, drain off the soaking water, and place the beans in a large pot or slow cooker. Cover with water, and stir in the dried garlic and onion, salt, bay leaf, sugar, cayenne pepper, celery seed, cumin, and crushed red pepper flakes. Push the ham hock down into the beans. Bring to a boil, reduce the heat, and simmer over low heat for 3 to 4 hours.
3. Stir in the smoked sausage, simmer for 20 more minutes, and serve.

G-MA'S RICE

Servings: 8 | Prep: 15m | Cooks: 30m | Total: 45m

NUTRITION FACTS

Calories: 207.8 | Carbohydrates: 38.9g | Protein: 3.8g | Cholesterol: 0mg | Sodium: 222.3mg

INGREDIENTS

- 2 tablespoons vegetable oil
- 2 cups long grain white rice
- 1 (8 ounce) can tomato sauce
- 1 teaspoon minced garlic

- 1/4 teaspoon salt

- 1 teaspoon black pepper

- 1 teaspoon ground cumin

- 4 cups water

DIRECTIONS

1. In a medium saucepan, heat vegetable oil over medium heat. Brown the rice in the oil until there is a golden texture, stirring frequently. Reduce heat to low, and stir in tomato sauce, garlic, salt, pepper, and cumin. Stir in water. Cover, and cook for about 20 minutes.

SAFFRON RICE

Servings: 6 | Prep: 15m | Cooks: 45m | Total: 1h

NUTRITION FACTS

Calories: 259.3 | Carbohydrates: 26.8g | Protein: 2.8g | Cholesterol: 40.7mg | Sodium: 113mg

INGREDIENTS

- 1/2 cup butter
- 1/4 cup diced onion
- 1 cup uncooked long grain white rice
- 2 cups water
- 1/2 teaspoon dried parsley flakes
- 1 pinch saffron threads
- 3 drops yellow food coloring

DIRECTIONS

1. Heat the butter in a saucepan over medium heat. Stir in the onion; cook and stir until the onion has softened and turned translucent, about 5 minutes. Reduce heat to medium-low, and continue cooking and stirring until the onion is very tender and dark brown, 15 to 20 minutes more.
2. Pour in rice and stir to coat. Stir in water, parsley flakes, saffron, and 3 drops of yellow food coloring (optional). Reduce heat, cover, and simmer until water is absorbed, about 30 minutes.

WILD RICE STUFFED ACORN SQUASH

Servings: 8 | Prep: 30m | Cooks: 1h | Total: 1h30m

NUTRITION FACTS

Calories: 187 | Carbohydrates: 39.2g | Fat: 2.1g | Protein: 5.1g | Cholesterol: 3mg | Sodium: 637mg

INGREDIENTS

- 2 acorn squash, halved and seeded
- 1 (6 ounce) package dry corn bread stuffing mix
- 2 teaspoons butter
- 1 onion, diced
- 1 clove garlic, minced
- 1 cup chopped fresh mushrooms
- 1 cup long grain and wild rice mix
- 2 sprigs fresh sage, chopped
- 2 cups vegetable stock
- 1 cup chopped fresh mushrooms

DIRECTIONS

1. Preheat an oven to 350 degrees F (175 degrees C). Lightly grease 2 baking pans, and place the cleaned-out squash, cut sides down, into the pans. Bake in the preheated oven until barely soft to the touch, about 25 minutes.
2. Make the stuffing mix as instructed on the package, and set aside.
3. Melt the butter over medium heat in a saucepan, and cook and stir the onion and garlic until the onion is translucent, about 10 minutes. Stir in the mushrooms, and cook and stir until they give up their juice, about 5 more minutes. Add the rice mix and sage, and cook and stir the rice and vegetables until the vegetables begin to brown, about 5 minutes. Pour in the vegetable stock, stir to combine, cover, and reduce heat. Simmer the rice mixture until tender, 30 to 40 minutes.
4. Lightly mix the cooked rice mixture with the stuffing in a bowl, and pile the mixture into the centers of the squash without packing it. Return the stuffed squash to the oven and bake until the squash are tender and the stuffing is hot, about 15 more minutes.

COPYCAT CHIPOTLE CILANTRO-LIME BROWN RICE

Servings: 4 | Prep: 10m | Cooks: 30m | Total: 45m | Additional: 5m

NUTRITION FACTS

Calories: 359.1 | Carbohydrates: 73.6g | Protein: 7.3g | Cholesterol: 0mg | Sodium: 453.9mg

INGREDIENTS

- 4 cups water
- 2 cups brown rice
- 1 lime, juiced
- 1 teaspoon minced garlic
- 1 teaspoon extra-virgin olive oil
- 1 teaspoon sea salt
- 1/2 cup chopped fresh cilantro

DIRECTIONS

1. Bring water and brown rice to a boil in a saucepan. Reduce heat to medium-low, cover, and simmer until rice is tender and liquid has been absorbed, 30 to 45 minutes.
2. Transfer brown rice to a large bowl and cool slightly, 5 to 7 minutes.
3. Whisk lime juice, garlic, olive oil, and salt together in a bowl; stir into rice. Fold cilantro into rice mixture.

MEXICAN TOMATO-FLAVORED RICE

Servings: 4 | Prep: 5m | Cooks: 25m | Total: 35m | Additional: 5m

NUTRITION FACTS

Calories: 240.4 | Carbohydrates: 39.7g | Protein: 3.8g | Cholesterol: 0mg | Sodium: 10.7mg

INGREDIENTS

- 2 tablespoons vegetable oil
- 1 cup long-grain rice
- 2 1/2 cups water
- 1 1/2 tablespoons tomato-flavored bouillon powder (such as Knorr)
- 2 dashes onion powder
- 2 dashes garlic powder

DIRECTIONS

1. Heat oil in a saucepan over medium heat. Fry rice in hot oil until golden brown, 2 to 3 minutes. Stream water into the saucepan while stirring the rice; season with tomato powder, onion powder, and garlic powder and stir.
2. Bring the mixture to a boil and cook at a boil for 2 minutes. Reduce heat to low, place a cover on the saucepan, and cook until the moisture is mostly absorbed by the rice, about 15 minutes. Remove saucepan from heat and let sit covered to let last moisture be absorbed into rice, about 5 minutes more.

BRAZILIAN RICE

Servings: 2 | Prep: 15m | Cooks: 25m | Total: 40m

NUTRITION FACTS

Calories: 474.3 | Carbohydrates: 77.9g | Protein: 7.2g | Cholesterol: 0mg | Sodium: 1178.7mg

INGREDIENTS

- 2 tablespoons olive oil
- 1/4 onion, diced
- 2 cloves garlic, minced
- 1 cup rice
- 2 cups water
- 4 sprigs fresh cilantro
- 1 teaspoon salt
- 3 drops lemon juice

DIRECTIONS

1. Heat oil in a saucepan over medium-low heat. Add onion and garlic; cook and stir until softened, about 5 minutes. Add rice and mix until clumps form.
2. Stir water, cilantro, salt, and lemon juice into the saucepan. Simmer uncovered until most of the water has been absorbed, about 10 minutes. Reduce heat, cover, and cook until rice is tender, 10 to 15 minutes.

ARANCINI

Servings: 18 | Prep: 20m | Cooks: 35m | Total: 55m

NUTRITION FACTS

Calories: 252.2 | Carbohydrates: 18.8g | Protein: 6.3g | Cholesterol: 29.1mg | Sodium: 274mg

INGREDIENTS

- 1 tablespoon olive oil
- 1 small onion, finely chopped
- 1 clove garlic, crushed
- 1 cup uncooked Arborio rice
- 1/2cup dry white wine
- 2 1/2cups boiling chicken stock
- 1/2cup frozen green peas
- 2 ounces finely chopped ham
- 1 pinch salt and pepper to taste

- 1/2 cup finely grated Parmesan cheese
- 1 egg, beaten
- 1 egg
- 1 tablespoon milk
- 4 ounces mozzarella cheese, cut into 3/4 inch cubes
- 1/2 cup all-purpose flour
- 1 cup dry bread crumbs
- 1 cup vegetable oil for deep frying

DIRECTIONS

1. Heat the olive oil in a large saucepan over medium heat. Add onion and garlic, and cook, stirring until onion is soft but not browned. Pour in the rice, and cook stirring for 2 minutes, then stir in the wine, and continue cooking and stirring until the liquid has evaporated. Add hot chicken stock to the rice 1/3 cup at a time, stirring and cooking until the liquid has evaporated before adding more.

2. When the chicken stock has all been added, and the liquid has evaporated, stir in the peas and ham. Season with salt and pepper. Remove from the heat, and stir in the Parmesan cheese. Transfer the risotto to a bowl, and allow to cool slightly.
3. Stir the beaten egg into the risotto. In a small bowl, whisk together the remaining egg and milk with a fork. For each ball, roll 2 tablespoons of the risotto into a ball. Press a piece of the mozzarella cheese into the center, and roll to enclose. Coat lightly with flour, dip into the milk mixture, then roll in bread crumbs to coat.
4. Heat oil for frying in a deep-fryer or large deep saucepan to 350 degrees F (175 degrees C). Fry the balls in small batches until evenly golden, turning as needed. Drain on paper towels. Keep warm in a low oven while the rest are frying.

MEXICAN RICE PILAF

Servings: 2 | Prep: 25m | Cooks: 10m | Total: 35m

NUTRITION FACTS

Calories: 590.3 | Carbohydrates: 68.5g | Protein: 23.2g | Cholesterol: 50.3mg | Sodium: 692.4mg

INGREDIENTS

- 1 tablespoon vegetable oil
- 1 onion, chopped
- 1 teaspoon minced garlic
- 1 1/2cups vegetable broth
- 1 1/2cups instant brown rice
- 2 teaspoons chili powder
- 1 jalapeno pepper, seeded and minced
- 1/2 teaspoon ground cumin
- 1 red bell pepper, chopped
- 1 large tomato, seeded and chopped
- 1 cup shredded Monterey Jack cheese

DIRECTIONS

1. In a large saucepan, heat oil over medium high heat. Add onion and garlic; cook for 3 minutes, stirring occasionally. Stir in broth, rice, chili powder, jalapeno peppers, and cumin. Cover, and bring to a boil over high heat. Reduce heat, and simmer for 4 minutes. Stir in bell pepper. Cover. Simmer for 5 minutes, or until liquid is absorbed.
2. Stir tomato and shredded cheese into hot cooked rice.

GARLIC RICE

Servings: 4 | Prep: 5m | Cooks: 5m | Total: 10m

NUTRITION FACTS

Calories: 293.4 | Carbohydrates: 45.9g | Protein: 5.9g | Cholesterol: 5.9mg | Sodium: 686.3mg

INGREDIENTS

- 2 tablespoons vegetable oil
- 1 1/2 tablespoons chopped garlic
- 2 tablespoons ground pork
- 4 cups cooked white rice
- 1 1/2 teaspoons garlic salt
- 1 pinch ground black pepper to taste

DIRECTIONS

1. Heat the oil in a large skillet over medium-high heat. When the oil is hot, add the garlic and ground pork. Cook and stir until the garlic is golden brown. This is the color you want for maximum flavor, do not allow it to burn, or the flavor will be bitter.
2. Stir in the cooked white rice, and season with garlic salt and pepper. Cook and stir until heated through and well blended, about 3 minutes. Serve and enjoy.

GREEN RICE

Servings: 6 | Prep: 10m | Cooks: 50m | Total: 1h

NUTRITION FACTS

Calories: 333.3 | Carbohydrates: 41g | Protein: 14.5g | Cholesterol: 69mg | Sodium: 229.2mg

INGREDIENTS

- 2 1/2 cups water
- 1 1/4 cups uncooked white rice
- 1 (10 ounce) package spinach, chopped
- 1 egg
- 1 (12 fluid ounce) can evaporated milk
- 1 cup shredded Cheddar cheese

DIRECTIONS

1. Preheat oven to 350 degrees F (175 degrees C). Lightly oil a 2 quart casserole dish.

2. In a saucepan, combine water and rice, and bring to a boil. Reduce heat, cover, and simmer for 20 minutes. Remove from heat, and stir in the spinach, egg, evaporated milk, and cheese. Spoon into the prepared casserole dish.
3. Bake for 30 minutes in the preheated oven, or until middle is set.

EASY MEXICAN RICE

Servings: 4 | Prep: 5m | Cooks: 1h | Total: 1h20m | Additional: 15m

NUTRITION FACTS

Calories: 361 | Carbohydrates: 72.3g | Protein: 12.2g | Cholesterol: 0mg | Sodium: 1459.4mg

INGREDIENTS

- 1 1/2 cups uncooked brown rice
- 3 cups water
- 1 (1 ounce) package taco seasoning mix
- 1 (15.25 ounce) can kidney beans, drained
- 1 (15 ounce) can tomato sauce
- 1 (14.5 ounce) can diced tomatoes, drained
- salt and pepper to taste
- 1/2 cup shredded lettuce

DIRECTIONS

1. In a saucepan bring 3 cups water to a boil. Add rice and stir. Reduce heat, cover and simmer for 45 minutes. Remove from heat and let stand for 15 minutes.
2. Stir in taco seasoning, kidney beans, tomato sauce, diced tomatoes, salt, pepper and lettuce.
3. Cook over medium heat until heated through.

PERSIAN RICE

Servings: 8 | Prep: 15m | Cooks: 55m | Total: 1h10m

NUTRITION FACTS

Calories: 255 | Carbohydrates: 41.6g | Protein: 4.2g | Cholesterol: 11mg | Sodium: 2223mg

INGREDIENTS

- 3 quarts water
- 3 tablespoons kosher salt
- 2 cups basmati rice,
- 1 russet potato, cut into 1/4-inch slices
- 3 tablespoons butter, cut into thin slices, or to taste
- 1 pinch saffron threads

rinsed

- 1 pinch ground cumin

- salt to taste

- 2 tablespoons olive oil

- 1 1/2 tablespoons hot water

- 1 tablespoon chopped parsley, or to taste

DIRECTIONS

1. Bring water and kosher salt to a boil in a pot; add rice and cook, stirring, for exactly 7 minutes. Drain.
2. Heat olive oil in a pot over medium-high heat. Cover bottom of pot with 1 layer of potato slices. Sprinkle cumin and salt over potatoes. Cook until potatoes are sizzling, 2 to 3 minutes; top potatoes with rice to form an even layer. Reduce heat to low and place butter slices over rice.
3. Top pot with a layer of clean paper towels and place lid over towels. Steam until rice is fluffy, about 45 minutes.
4. Grind saffron threads with a mortar and pestle. Mix crushed saffron with 1 1/2 tablespoons hot water in a large bowl. Add a couple spoonfuls of rice to saffron mixture and stir until rice is yellow.
5. Spoon remaining rice into a serving bowl, top with saffron rice, and line edges of bowl with potatoes. Garnish with parsley.

ANN'S RICE PILAF

Servings: 4 | Prep: 5m | Cooks: 30m | Total: 35m

NUTRITION FACTS

Calories: 357.1 | Carbohydrates: 54g | Protein: 6.7g | Cholesterol: 30.6mg | Sodium: 1122.7mg

INGREDIENTS

- 2 teaspoons chicken bouillon granules

- 2 cups water

- 1/4 cup butter

- 3/4 cup broken pieces vermicelli pasta

- 1 cup long grain white rice

- 1 teaspoon freshly ground black pepper

- 1/2 teaspoon salt

- 1/4 teaspoon Greek seasoning, or to taste

DIRECTIONS

1. Dissolve chicken bouillon in water in a bowl.
2. Melt butter in a skillet over medium-high heat. Cook and stir vermicelli pieces until golden brown, about 5 minutes.

3. Pour bouillon mixture into the skillet with the vermicelli.
4. Stir rice, black pepper, salt, and Greek seasoning into the vermicelli mixture and bring to a boil. Cover and reduce heat to low; simmer until rice is tender and liquid is absorbed, 20 to 25 minutes.

INSTANT POT MEXICAN RICE

Servings: 4 | Prep: 10m | Cooks: 20m | Total: 35m | Additional: 5m

NUTRITION FACTS

Calories: 224.6 | Carbohydrates: 41.1g | Protein: 5.2g | Cholesterol: 1.5mg | Sodium: 787.7mg

INGREDIENTS

- 1 tablespoon avocado oil, or more as needed
- 1/2 medium onion, finely chopped
- 2 large cloves garlic, minced
- 1 cup long-grain rice
- 1 1/2 cups low-sodium chicken stock
- 1/2 cup tomato sauce
- 1 teaspoon salt
- 1/4 teaspoon ground cumin
- 1 pinch cayenne pepper

DIRECTIONS

1. Turn on a multi-functional pressure cooker (such as Instant Pot®); select Saute function and adjust to medium. Cover the bottom of the pot with avocado oil. Cook and stir onion until soft, 4 to 5 minutes. Add garlic and cook until fragrant, about 30 seconds.
2. Add rice to the pot and mix until coated with oil and lightly browned. Pour in chicken stock; stir any browned bits off the bottom of the pot. Mix in tomato sauce, salt, cumin, and cayenne pepper. Close and lock the lid. Seal the vent and select high pressure function. Set timer for 7 minutes; allow 10 to 15 minutes for pressure to build.
3. Release pressure carefully using the quick-release method according to manufacturer's instructions, about 5 minutes. Unlock and remove the lid. Stir rice before serving.

ARROZ ROJO (MEXICAN RED RICE)

Servings: 5 | Prep: 15m | Cooks: 25m | Total: 50m | Additional: 10m

NUTRITION FACTS

Calories: 213.3 | Carbohydrates: 35.1g | Protein: 4.6g | Cholesterol: 1.4mg | Sodium: 108.7mg

INGREDIENTS

- 2 Roma (plum tomatoes), cored
- 2 tablespoons vegetable oil
- 1 cup minced onion
- 2 cloves garlic, minced
- 1 cup uncooked long-grain white rice

- 1 3/4 cups low-sodium chicken broth
- 1/4 cup canned tomato sauce
- 1 jalapeno pepper, chopped
- 2 sprigs fresh cilantro
- 1 pinch salt to taste

DIRECTIONS

1. Grate tomatoes into a bowl using a box grater; discard tomato skins.
2. Heat vegetable oil in a heavy skillet over medium-high heat and cook onion until translucent, stirring often, about 5 minutes. Stir garlic into onion and cook until fragrant, about 1 minute.
3. Stir rice into onion mixture and cook, stirring often, until rice is lightly toasted, about 3 more minutes. Stir grated tomato, chicken broth, and tomato sauce into the rice. Bring mixture to a boil.
4. Mix in jalapeno pepper, cilantro, and salt; reduce heat to low. Cover skillet and simmer until rice has absorbed the liquid, about 15 minutes. Do not lift the cover while the rice is cooking.
5. Turn off heat and let rice stand covered for 8 minutes. Fluff with a fork before transferring rice to a serving dish.

STOVETOP SAFFRON RICE

Servings: 5 | Prep: 10m | Cooks: 40m | Total: 1h20m | Additional: 30m

NUTRITION FACTS

Calories: 404 | Carbohydrates: 69.5g | Protein: 7.1g | Cholesterol: 24.4mg | Sodium: 811.9mg

INGREDIENTS

- 2 cups uncooked long-grain rice
- 3/4 teaspoon crushed saffron threads
- 4 tablespoons butter
- 6 whole cardamom seeds
- 4 eaches whole cloves

- 3 cinnamon sticks
- 1 onion, chopped
- 3 cups boiling vegetable broth
- 1 teaspoon salt

DIRECTIONS

1. Cover rice with cold water and set aside to soak for 30 minutes.
2. Soak saffron threads in 2 tablespoons boiling water.
3. Melt butter in a large saucepan over medium heat; add cardamom, cloves and cinnamon and fry 2 minutes, stirring occasionally. Stir in onion and saute, stirring occasionally, until golden brown. Stir in the rice, reduce heat to low and simmer for 5 minutes, stirring constantly.
4. Pour in the boiling broth and stir in the salt and saffron.
5. Cover and cook until rice is cooked and all liquid is absorbed, about 40 minutes.

LESLIE'S BROCCOLI, WILD RICE, AND MUSHROOM STUFFING

Servings: 12 | Prep: 15m | Cooks: 1h5m | Total: 1h30m

NUTRITION FACTS

Calories: 271 | Carbohydrates: 35.9g | Protein: 7g | Cholesterol: 21.1mg | Sodium: 738.6mg

INGREDIENTS

- 1/2cup uncooked wild rice
- 1 1/2cups water
- 2 cups chopped fresh broccoli
- 1/2cup butter
- 1 1/2cups sliced mushrooms
- 1 cup chopped onion
- 1 (16 ounce) package herb seasoned stuffing mix
- 1 (14 ounce) can chicken broth
- 1/2 cup sliced almonds

DIRECTIONS

1. Bring rice and 1 1/2 cups water to boil in a pot. Cover, reduce heat to low, and simmer 45 minutes.
2. Place broccoli in a pot with enough water to cover, and boil 5 minutes, or until slightly tender. Remove from heat, and drain.
3. Preheat oven to 350 degrees F (175 degrees C). Lightly grease a baking dish.
4. Melt the butter in a skillet over medium heat, and saute the mushrooms and onion until tender. Mix in cooked rice, cooked broccoli, stuffing mix, broth, and almonds. Transfer to the prepared baking dish (or use to stuff turkey just before roasting).
5. Bake 30 minutes in the preheated oven, or until golden brown.

MAMACITA'S MEXICAN RICE

Servings: 6 | Prep: 10m | Cooks: 25m | Total: 35m

NUTRITION FACTS

Calories: 156.3 | Carbohydrates: 29.6g | Protein: 34.1g | Cholesterol: 0mg | Sodium: 34.1mg

INGREDIENTS

- 1 cup long-grain white rice
- 1 tablespoon vegetable oil
- 1 onion, minced
- 1 clove garlic, minced
- 1 1/2 cups chicken broth
- 1 tomato, seeded and diced
- 1/2 teaspoon ground cumin
- 1/2 teaspoon Spanish saffron
- 1 pinch salt and ground black pepper to taste
- 1/4 cup frozen peas and carrots, thawed
- 1 sprig fresh cilantro

DIRECTIONS

1. Cook and stir rice and oil in a skillet over medium heat until lightly toasted, about 2 minutes. Add onion and cook for 2 minutes. Add garlic and cook until fragrant, about 1 minute.
2. Pour chicken broth into rice mixture and bring to a boil; stir tomato, cumin, saffron, salt, and black pepper into broth and bring to a boil. Cover, reduce heat to low, and simmer until rice is cooked, about 20 minutes.
3. Stir peas and carrots into cooked rice; garnish with cilantro.

EASY AUTHENTIC SPANISH RICE

Servings: 8 | Prep: 10m | Cooks: 45m | Total: 55m

NUTRITION FACTS

Calories: 253 | Carbohydrates: 26.7g | Protein: 5.2g | Cholesterol: 36.6mg | Sodium: 521.7mg

INGREDIENTS

- 6 tablespoons butter
- 2 onions, chopped
- 1 cup uncooked white rice
- 1 pinch salt and ground black pepper to taste

- 2 jalapeno peppers, chopped
- 2 (14.5 ounce) cans Mexican-style diced tomatoes, undrained
- 1/2 cup sour cream, or as desired
- 1/2 cup shredded Cheddar cheese, or as desired

DIRECTIONS

1. Melt butter in a large skillet over medium-high heat; cook and stir onions and jalapeno peppers in the butter until softened, 3 to 5 minutes. Stir Mexican-style tomatoes into onion mixture; add rice, salt, and black pepper. Bring rice mixture to a boil, reduce heat, cover, and simmer until rice is cooked, 40 to 45 minutes. Garnish with sour cream and Cheddar cheese to serve.

SPANISH RICE

Servings: 4 | Prep: 5m | Cooks: 15m | Total: 20m

NUTRITION FACTS

Calories: 508.8 | Carbohydrates: 108.4g | Protein: 10.8g | Cholesterol: 0mg | Sodium: 684mg

INGREDIENTS

- 1 tablespoon vegetable oil
- 1 1/2cups instant rice
- 1 onion, chopped
- 1 red bell pepper, chopped
- 1/2 green bell pepper, chopped
- 1 teaspoon prepared mustard
- 1/2teaspoon salt
- 1 1/2 (14.5 ounce) cans whole peeled tomatoes
- 1 cup tomato juice

DIRECTIONS

1. In a large saucepan over medium heat combine oil, rice, onion, red bell pepper and green bell pepper. Saute until onions are translucent. Stir in mustard, salt, tomatoes and tomato juice; simmer for 5 minutes.

OKRA RICE

Servings: 6 | Prep: 15m | Cooks: 45m | Total: 1h

NUTRITION FACTS

Calories: 280.8 | Carbohydrates: 32.3g | Protein: 13g | Cholesterol: 27.5mg | Sodium: 582.7mg

INGREDIENTS

- 1 pound bacon - cooked and crumbled
- 1 large onion, chopped
- 3 cups sliced fresh or frozen okra
- 1 (14.5 ounce) can chicken broth
- 1 cup uncooked rice
- 1 1/2 cups water

DIRECTIONS

1. Place bacon in a large, deep skillet. Cook over medium high heat until evenly brown. Drain grease and set aside for later use. Crumble bacon and set aside.
2. In the same skillet, saute onion in a small amount of reserved bacon grease over medium high heat until tender, about 3 minutes. Add crumbled bacon, sliced okra, and chicken broth. Reduce heat and simmer until okra is tender and falling apart, about 15 minutes. Stir in rice and water. Cover, and simmer for 20 minutes, or until fluffy.

EASY CILANTRO-LIME RICE

Servings: 6 | Prep: 15m | Cooks: 20m | Total: 35m

NUTRITION FACTS

Calories: 143.7 | Carbohydrates: 27.1g | Protein: 3g | Cholesterol: 1.3mg | Sodium: 650.2mg

INGREDIENTS

- 1 tablespoon olive oil
- 1 cup basmati rice
- 2 cloves garlic, minced
- 1 1/2 cups chicken broth
- 2 tablespoons fresh lime juice
- 1 teaspoon salt
- 1/2 cup chopped cilantro
- 1/4 cup whole-kernel corn
- 2 teaspoons green onions, chopped
- 1 lime, zested

DIRECTIONS

1. Heat olive oil in a saucepan over medium heat. Cook and stir rice and garlic in hot oil until fragrant, about 2 minutes. Stir chicken broth, lime juice, and salt into rice; bring to a boil, reduce heat to medium-low, cover the saucepan with a lid, and simmer until rice is tender and liquid is absorbed, about 15 minutes.
2. Stir cilantro, corn, green onions, and lime zest into rice until well-mixed.

RAISIN AND SPICE BROWN RICE
Servings: 7 | Prep: 10m | Cooks: 45m | Total: 55m

NUTRITION FACTS

Calories: 161.3 | Carbohydrates: 28.2g | Protein: 2.7g | Cholesterol: 4.4mg | Sodium: 95.4mg

INGREDIENTS

- 1 cup brown rice
- 2 cups chicken broth
- 1 tablespoon butter
- 1 bay leaf
- 1 tablespoon vegetable oil
- 1 cup chopped onion
- 1 teaspoon minced fresh ginger
- 1 teaspoon ground cumin
- 1/2 teaspoon ground coriander
- 1/3 cup thinly sliced celery
- 1/4 cup seedless raisins
- 1 tablespoon low-sodium soy sauce
- 1 pinch freshly ground black pepper to taste

DIRECTIONS

1. Bring brown rice, chicken broth, butter, and bay leaf to a boil in a saucepan over high heat. Reduce heat to medium-low, cover, and simmer until the rice is tender, 45 to 50 minutes; discard bay leaf.
2. Meanwhile, heat the vegetable oil in a skillet over medium-high heat. Stir in onion and ginger; cook and stir until the onion begins to brown on the edges, about 3 minutes. Stir in the cumin and coriander, then stir in the celery and raisins. Reduce heat to medium, and cook until the celery becomes tender, about 5 minutes. Once ready, stir the onion mixture into the cooked rice along with the soy sauce; season to taste with pepper.

EASY SPICED BROWN RICE WITH CORN

Servings: 6 | Prep: 5m | Cooks: 1h | Total: 1h5m

NUTRITION FACTS

Calories: 133.4 | Carbohydrates: 24.4g | Protein: 2.7g | Cholesterol: 0mg | Sodium: 198.3mg

INGREDIENTS

- 2 cups water
- 1 cup brown rice
- 1 tablespoon olive oil
- 1/2teaspoon salt
- 1 cup frozen corn kernels
- 1/2teaspoon dried cilantro
- 1/2 teaspoon cumin seed

DIRECTIONS

1. In a saucepan, mix the water, rice, olive oil, and salt, and bring to a boil. Mix in the corn, cilantro, and cumin. Reduce heat, cover, and simmer 45 to 60 minutes, until the liquid has been absorbed.

MINNESOTA WILD RICE DRESSING

Servings: 12 | Prep: 45m | Cooks: 15m | Total: 1h

NUTRITION FACTS

Calories: 417.9 | Carbohydrates: 20.4g | Protein: 12.7g | Cholesterol: 82.5mg | Sodium: 834.9mg

INGREDIENTS

- 2 (4.5 ounce) packages instant long grain and wild rice
- 1 (16 ounce) package ground pork sausage
- 1 (16 ounce) package ground sage pork sausage
- 1/2 cup chopped celery
- 1 medium onion, chopped
- 1/2 pound fresh mushrooms, sliced
- 1 (5 ounce) can water chestnuts, drained and sliced
- 1/4 teaspoon garlic powder
- 2 eggs, beaten

DIRECTIONS

1. Prepare instant long grain and wild rice according to package directions. Preheat oven to 350 degrees F (175 degrees C). Lightly grease a 9x13 inch baking dish.
2. Place ground pork sausage and ground sage pork sausage in a large, deep skillet. Cook over medium high heat until evenly brown. Drain, and set aside. Cook and stir celery, onion, mushrooms, and water chestnuts in the skillet until browned and tender. Season with garlic powder.
3. Mix prepared rice, sausage, celery mixture, and eggs in the prepared baking dish. Bake 15 minutes in the preheated oven, until lightly browned.

EGGPLANT AND MUSHROOMS WITH WILD RICE

Servings: 6 | Prep: 10m | Cooks: 30m | Total: 40m

NUTRITION FACTS

Calories: 242.8 | Carbohydrates: 17.7g | Protein: 4.7g | Cholesterol: 22.7mg | Sodium: 576mg

INGREDIENTS

- 3 tablespoons butter
- 3 tablespoons olive oil, divided
- 1 large eggplant, peeled and cubed
- 1 medium onion, chopped
- 8 ounces fresh mushrooms, sliced
- 1/2teaspoon minced garlic
- 1/2teaspoon salt
- 1/4 teaspoon ground black pepper
- 1 teaspoon Italian seasoning
- 1 cup chicken broth
- 1 (10.75 ounce) can condensed cream of mushroom soup
- 1/2 cup half-and-half or light cream
- 1 cup cooked wild rice

DIRECTIONS

1. Heat butter and 1 tablespoon of olive oil in a large skillet. Add the eggplant, and fry until tender, about 5 minutes. Remove eggplant from the skillet, and keep warm.
2. Add the remaining 2 tablespoons of olive oil to the skillet, and fry the onion and mushrooms until tender, about 5 minutes. Return the eggplant to the pan, and season with garlic, salt, pepper, and Italian seasoning. Cook and stir for one minute to blend the flavors.
3. Stir in the chicken broth, and simmer for about 5 minutes, until most of the liquid is reduced or absorbed. Stir in cream of mushroom soup, half-and-half cream, and cooked wild rice. Simmer over

low heat for 15 minutes, stirring occasionally. Taste and adjust seasoning with salt and pepper if desired.

KE'S CAJUN (DIRTY) RICE

Servings: 6 | Prep: 15m | Cooks: 1h | Total: 1h15m

NUTRITION FACTS

Calories: 141 | Carbohydrates: 18.1g | Protein: 9.4g | Cholesterol: 27.9mg | Sodium: 106.6mg

INGREDIENTS

- 1 1/2cups water
- 2/3 cup uncooked brown rice
- 1/2pound ground turkey
- 1/2cup chopped green bell pepper
- 1/3 cup chopped onion
- 1/2teaspoon minced garlic
- 1/2 teaspoon garlic powder
- 1/2teaspoon dried celery flakes
- 1 teaspoon Cajun seasoning
- 1/4 teaspoon ground black pepper
- 1/3 cup water
- 1 pinch salt, or to taste

DIRECTIONS

1. Bring 1 1/2 cup of water to a boil in a saucepan, and stir in the brown rice. Reduce the heat to a simmer, cover, and simmer until the rice is tender and the liquid has been absorbed, 40 to 50 minutes. Set the rice aside.
2. Place ground turkey into a skillet over medium heat, and cook and stir the turkey until the meat gives up some of its fat, 2 to 3 minutes; stir in green bell pepper, onion, and minced garlic. Cook and stir until the turkey is crumbly and no longer pink and the vegetables are tender, 5 to 8 more minutes. Drain excess grease, if necessary. Stir in the cooked brown rice, garlic powder, celery flakes, Cajun seasoning, black pepper, and 1/3 cup water.
3. Bring the mixture to a simmer, and cook until the liquid is absorbed, about 10 minutes. Season to taste with salt and additional black pepper, if desired.

SOUTH AFRICAN YELLOW RICE

Servings: 4 | Prep: 10m | Cooks: 35m | Total: 45m

NUTRITION FACTS

Calories: 295.8 | Carbohydrates: 63.5g | Protein: 4g | Cholesterol: 7.6mg | Sodium: 316.1mg

INGREDIENTS

- 1 cup long grain white rice
- 1/2 teaspoon salt
- 1 1/2 teaspoons ground turmeric
- 3 tablespoons white sugar
- 1/2 teaspoon ground cinnamon
- 1/2 cup black raisins
- 1 tablespoon butter
- 2 1/2 cups water

DIRECTIONS

1. In a saucepan, combine the rice, salt, turmeric, sugar, cinnamon, raisins, butter and water. Bring to a boil uncovered. When it comes to a boil, reduce the heat to low, cover and let it simmer for 20 to 30 minutes, or until rice is fluffy and water has been absorbed. Remove from the heat and fluff with a fork. Keep warm until serving time.

FAIRY GODMOTHER RICE

Servings: 6 | Prep: 15m | Cooks: 45m | Total: 1h

NUTRITION FACTS

Calories: 402.4 | Carbohydrates: 54.5g | Protein: 6.7g | Cholesterol: 57.6mg | Sodium: 1249.5mg

INGREDIENTS

- 1/2 cup butter
- 5 ounces thin egg noodles
- 2 cups uncooked instant rice
- 2 (1 ounce) packages dry onion soup mix
- 4 cups vegetable broth
- 1 (5 ounce) can water chestnuts, drained and sliced
- soy sauce to taste

DIRECTIONS

1. Preheat oven to 350 degrees F (175 degrees C). Grease a 2 quart casserole dish.
2. Melt butter in a large skillet over medium heat. Brown noodles in the butter.
3. In a large bowl combine browned noodles, rice, soup mix, broth, water chestnuts and soy sauce. Mix well and transfer to prepared casserole dish.
4. Bake for 45 minutes, or until liquid has been absorbed and casserole is browned and crispy on top.

SPICY SPANISH-STYLE RICE

Servings: 8 | Prep: 10m | Cooks: 25m | Total: 45m

NUTRITION FACTS

Calories: 194 | Carbohydrates: 39.1g | Fat: 2.1g | Protein: 3.9g | Cholesterol: 4mg | Sodium: 436mg

INGREDIENTS

- 1 tablespoon butter
- 2 cups uncooked long-grain white rice
- 1/3 cup diced jalapeno pepper
- 1/3 cup chopped green onion
- 1 clove garlic, crushed
- 1 teaspoon chili powder, or to taste

- 1 teaspoon ground cumin
- 1/2 teaspoon salt
- 1/2 teaspoon chipotle chile powder, or to taste
- 1/2 teaspoon cayenne pepper, or to taste (optional)
- 2 1/4 cups chicken stock
- 1/2 cup tomato sauce

DIRECTIONS

1. Melt butter in a pot over medium-low heat. Stir rice, jalapeno, green onion, and garlic together in the melted butter until rice is completely coated with butter. Add chili powder, cumin, salt, chipotle chile powder, and cayenne pepper; cook and stir until fragrant, about 1 minute. Watch Now
2. Stir chicken stock and tomato sauce into rice mixture. Bring to a simmer, cover the pot, reduce heat to low, and simmer for 20 minutes. Turn heat off and leave pot covered on the burner for 8 minutes. Remove cover and fluff rice with a fork. Watch Now.

FRESH MUSHROOM RICE PILAF

Servings: 4 | Prep: 10m | Cooks: 20m | Total: 30m

NUTRITION FACTS

Calories: 149.5 | Carbohydrates: 27.8g | Protein: 4.2g | Cholesterol: 5.4mg | Sodium: 185mg

INGREDIENTS

- 2 teaspoons butter
- 1 (8 ounce) package sliced fresh mushrooms

- 2/3 cup white rice
- 1 teaspoon chicken bouillon granules

- 1/4 cup chopped green pepper
- 2 tablespoons chopped onion
- 1 1/3 cups water
- 1/8 teaspoon salt
- 1 pinch garlic powder
- 1 pinch ground black pepper

DIRECTIONS

1. Melt butter in a saucepan over medium heat; cook and stir mushrooms, bell pepper, and onion until tender, about 5 minutes. Stir in water, rice, bouillon granules, salt, garlic powder, and black pepper. Bring to a boil; reduce heat to medium-low, cover, and simmer until liquid is absorbed and rice is tender, 14 to 16 minutes.

SARAH'S FETA RICE PILAF

Servings: 4 | Prep: 10m | Cooks: 30m | Total: 40m

NUTRITION FACTS

Calories: 295.2 | Carbohydrates: 41g | Protein: 8.8g | Cholesterol: 34.5mg | Sodium: 739.5mg

INGREDIENTS

- 2 tablespoons butter
- 1/2cup orzo pasta
- 1/2cup diced onion
- 2 cloves garlic, minced
- 1/2 cup white rice
- 2 cups chicken broth
- 1 cup chopped spinach
- 1/2cup chopped Bulgarian feta cheese

DIRECTIONS

1. Melt butter in a skillet over medium-low heat; cook and stir oro in the melted butter until golden brown, 3 to 5 minutes. Stir onion into orzo and cook until translucent, 5 to 10 minutes. Cook and stir garlic into orzo-onion mixture until fragrant, about 1 minute.
2. Mix rice and chicken broth into orzo-onion mixture; bring to a boil. Reduce heat to medium-low, cover skillet, and simmer until rice is tender and liquid is absorbed, 20 to 25 minutes. Remove from heat and stir in spinach and feta. Cover and let stand until spinach is wilted and feta is melted, about 5 minutes. Fluff with a fork.

CRANBERRY AND ALMOND RICE PILAF

Servings: 8 | Prep: 15m | Cooks: 30m | Total: 45m

NUTRITION FACTS

Calories: 212.6 | Carbohydrates: 39.4g | Protein: 5.1g | Cholesterol: 1.5mg | Sodium: 285.2mg

INGREDIENTS

- 1 tablespoon olive oil
- 3/4 cup chopped onions
- 1/2 cup dried cranberries
- 1 1/2 cups uncooked jasmine rice
- 3 cups low-sodium chicken broth
- 1 teaspoon kosher salt, or to taste
- 1 pinch ground black pepper to taste
- 2 green onions, chopped
- 3 tablespoons chopped fresh cilantro
- 1/4 cup slivered almonds

DIRECTIONS

1. Heat olive oil in a large skillet or Dutch oven over medium heat. Cook and stir onion in hot oil until tender and translucent, about 5 minutes.
2. Stir cranberries and jasmine rice into onion until rice is coated with oil and rice is lightly toasted, about 5 minutes more.
3. Pour chicken broth into skillet and season with kosher salt and black pepper.
4. Bring rice mixture to a boil over high heat, then cover and reduce heat to low. Simmer until rice is tender and liquid is absorbed, about 22 minutes.
5. Remove skillet from heat; stir green onions, cilantro, and almonds into rice mixture. Adjust seasoning if necessary.

LEMON DILL RICE

Servings: 8 | Prep: 10m | Cooks: 1h | Total: 1h10m

NUTRITION FACTS

Calories: 221.5 | Carbohydrates: 40.3g | Protein: 3.8g | Cholesterol: 11.4mg | Sodium: 1781.9mg

INGREDIENTS

- 3 tablespoons butter
- 1 large onion, minced
- 2 tablespoons salt
- 2 tablespoons dill seed

- 2 cups long-grain white rice
- 4 cups water
- 1/4 cup fresh lemon juice
- 1/2 teaspoon grated lemon zest
- 1 teaspoon chopped fresh parsley for garnish

DIRECTIONS

1. Preheat the oven to 325 degrees F (165 degrees C).
2. Melt butter in a heavy skillet over medium heat. Add the onion and rice; cook and stir until lightly toasted. Stir in the water and lemon juice, and season with salt and dill seed. Bring to a boil. Pour the rice mixture into a 3 quart casserole dish.
3. Bake for 1 hour, covered, in the preheated oven. Garnish with lemon zest and chopped parsley.

RICE STUFFING WITH APPLES, HERBS, AND BACON

Servings: 12 | Prep: 20m | Cooks: 1h10m | Total: 1h30m

NUTRITION FACTS

Calories: 313 | Carbohydrates: 59.2g | Fat: 6.4g | Protein: 7.2g | Cholesterol: 9mg | Sodium: 186mg

INGREDIENTS

- 3 1/2 cups water, divided
- 1 1/2 cups low fat, low sodium chicken broth
- 1 cup uncooked wild rice
- 1/3 pound bacon
- 3 cups diced onions
- 3 cups diced celery
- 1 tablespoon water
- 1 cup uncooked long-grain white rice
- 1 3/4 cups currants
- 3/4 cup dried cherries
- 3/4 cup dried cranberries
- 1/2 ounce dried apricots
- 1 cup diced, unpeeled apples
- 1/2 cup chopped Italian flat leaf parsley
- 6 tablespoons dried mixed herbs

DIRECTIONS

1. In a medium saucepan over medium heat, bring 1 1/2 cups water and the chicken broth to a boil. Stir in wild rice. Cover, reduce heat, and simmer 45 minutes.

2. Place bacon in a large, deep skillet. Cook over medium high heat until evenly brown. Reserving drippings, drain bacon, crumble, and set aside.
3. In the skillet with the reserved bacon drippings, saute onions and celery with 1 tablespoon water. Cook until very soft, about 20 minutes.
4. Stir remaining water, white rice, currants, cherries, cranberries, apricots, and apples into the wild rice. Continue cooking 20 minutes, or until wild rice and white rice are tender.
5. In a large bowl, mix the bacon and the onion mixture into the rice mixture. Season with the Italian parsley and dried mixed herbs.

SAVORY COCONUT RICE

Servings: 4 | Prep: 10m | Cooks: 22m | Total: 37m | Additional: 5m

NUTRITION FACTS

Calories: 535.1 | Carbohydrates: 67.1g | Protein: 7.6g | Cholesterol: 0mg | Sodium: 500mg

INGREDIENTS

- 1 1/2 cups jasmine or long-grain white rice
- 1 teaspoon finely grated fresh ginger
- 1/2 teaspoon red chili flakes
- 1/4 teaspoon ground turmeric
- 1 teaspoon kosher salt
- 1 cup water
- 1 (14 ounce) can coconut milk (not coconut cream)
- 1 bay leaf
- 1/4 cup toasted coconut for garnish

DIRECTIONS

1. Place rice in a heavy-bottomed saucepan. Add grated ginger, kosher salt, red chili flakes, and turmeric. Pour in water and coconut milk. Whisk until mixture is well combined (do not stir again).
2. Place pan over medium-high heat and bring to a simmer. When mixture starts to bubble and reaches a low simmer, place bay leaf on the surface, cover tightly, and reduce heat to low. Cook for 18 minutes without taking off the lid. Remove pan from heat and let sit 5 minutes, covered. Fluff rice with a fork.

ASPARAGUS-ZUCCHINI RICE

Servings: 4 | Prep: 15m | Cooks: 30m | Total: 45m

NUTRITION FACTS

Calories: 210 | Carbohydrates: 43.1g | Protein: 5.2g | Cholesterol: 3.8mg | Sodium: 23.1mg

INGREDIENTS

- 1/2tablespoon butter
- 1 onion, chopped
- 10 spears fresh asparagus, trimmed and cut into 2 inch pieces
- 1 zucchini, sliced
- 1/2 teaspoon dried oregano
- 1/2teaspoon dried basil
- 1/4 teaspoon dried thyme
- 1/8 teaspoon garlic powder
- 1 pinch cayenne pepper
- salt and pepper to taste
- 2 cups water
- 1 cup uncooked long-grain white rice

DIRECTIONS

1. In a medium saucepan over medium heat, melt the butter and saute the onion for about 2 minutes. Stir in asparagus and zucchini, and saute 5 minutes, or until tender. Season with oregano, basil, thyme, garlic powder, cayenne pepper, salt, and pepper. Cook and stir until vegetables are coated with the seasonings.
2. Pour water into the vegetable mixture, and stir in rice. Reduce heat, cover, and simmer 20 minutes, until the rice is tender.

BECKY'S EASY CILANTRO LIME RICE
Servings: 12 | Prep: 15m | Cooks: 30m | Total: 45m

NUTRITION FACTS

Calories: 114.5 | Carbohydrates: 22.8g | Protein: 2.2g | Cholesterol: 2.6mg | Sodium: 440.6mg

INGREDIENTS

- 1/2 onion, chopped
- 1 (4 ounce) can green chilies
- 1 tablespoon minced garlic
- 1 lime, juiced
- 1/2 bunch cilantro, chopped
- 3 cups water
- 4 teaspoons chicken bouillon granules
- 1 teaspoon salt
- 1 tablespoon butter, softened
- 3 cups uncooked instant rice

DIRECTIONS

1. Blend the onion, green chiles, garlic, and lime juice together in a food processor until smooth; add the cilantro and pulse until the cilantro is finely chopped into the mixture.
2. Bring the water to boil in a saucepan. Stir the cilantro mixture, chicken bouillon granules, salt, butter, and rice into the water and return to a boil; reduce heat to medium-low and cover. Simmer until the rice has absorbed the liquid entirely, about 20 minutes.

MAGNIFICENT CHEESY BROWN RICE

Servings: 8 | Prep: 10m | Cooks: 45m | Total: 55m

NUTRITION FACTS

Calories: 94.6 | Carbohydrates: 15g | Protein: 4.9g | Cholesterol: 3mg | Sodium: 87.5mg

INGREDIENTS

- 2 cups water
- 1 cup brown rice
- 1/2 red bell peppers, seeded and chopped
- 1/4 red onion, chopped
- 1 cup shredded low-fat Cheddar cheese

DIRECTIONS

1. Bring the brown rice, and water to a boil in a saucepan. Reduce the heat to medium-low, cover, and simmer until the rice is tender and the liquid has been absorbed, 45 to 50 minutes.
2. Prepare a skillet with cooking spray and place over medium heat. Cook the bell pepper and onion until lightly browned; stir into the cooked rice. Add the Cheddar cheese and continue stirring until the cheese has melted completely.

CARROTY RICE

Servings: 6 | Prep: 5m | Cooks: 25m | Total: 30m

NUTRITION FACTS

Calories: 125.4 | Carbohydrates: 27.1g | Protein: 2.7g | Cholesterol: 0.1mg | Sodium: 198.8mg

INGREDIENTS

- 2 cups water
- 1 carrot, shredded
- 1 cube chicken bouillon
- 1 cup uncooked long-grain rice

DIRECTIONS

1. Bring water to a boil in a medium saucepan over medium-high heat. Drop in bouillon cube and let dissolve. Stir in carrots and rice and return to boiling.
2. Reduce heat to low, cover and simmer for 20 minutes.
3. Remove from heat and let stand, covered, for 5 minutes.

VEGETABLE FETA RICE

Servings: 4 | Prep: 30m | Cooks: 40m | Total: 1h10m

NUTRITION FACTS

Calories: 384 | Carbohydrates: 62.6g | Protein: 9.9g | Cholesterol: 25.2mg | Sodium: 344mg

INGREDIENTS

- 1 1/2 cups uncooked long-grain white rice
- 3 cups water
- 1 cup chopped red onion
- 1 cup chopped celery
- 1 cup chopped cucumber
- 4 ounces feta cheese
- 1 tablespoon olive oil
- 2 tablespoons red wine vinegar

DIRECTIONS

1. Place rice and water in a medium-size pot. Bring water to a boil, when boiled reduce heat to a simmer, cover pot and let rice cook until tender.
2. In a large mixing bowl, combine red onion, celery, and cucumber. Crumble the feta into the bowl. Cover the vegetable mixture with cooked rice, cover and let sit for 5 minutes.
3. Toss vegetable and feta with oil and vinegar, and serve.

MEXICAN WHITE RICE

Servings: 6 | Prep: 20m | Cooks: 30m | Total: 50m

NUTRITION FACTS

Calories: 227.6 | Carbohydrates: 34.7g | Protein: 5.3g | Cholesterol: 13.6mg | Sodium: 249mg

INGREDIENTS

- 1 tablespoon vegetable oil
- 1/4 cup minced carrot

- 1/2 cup fresh corn kernels
- 1 fresh poblano chile pepper - seeded, deveined, and chopped
- 1/2 onion, chopped
- 1/4 cup drained canned peas
- 1 clove garlic, minced
- 1 cup water
- 1 cup milk
- 2 tablespoons butter
- 1 cup white rice, rinsed and drained
- 1 tablespoon chicken bouillon granules

DIRECTIONS

1. Heat the oil in a large saucepan over medium-high heat; cook the corn kernels in the hot oil until tender, about 5 minutes. Stir the poblano pepper, onion, peas, garlic, and carrot into the corn; cook and stir another 5 minutes.
2. Pour the water and milk into the mixture; bring to a boil. Allow the butter to melt into the boiling mixture. Add the rice and stir. Season with chicken bouillon; cover the saucepan, reduce heat to medium-low, and simmer the mixture until all the liquid is absorbed and the rice is tender, about 20 minutes.

QUICK AND EASY SPANISH RICE

Servings: 6 | Prep: 10m | Cooks: 25m | Total: 35m

NUTRITION FACTS

Calories: 235.1 | Carbohydrates: 42.4g | Protein: 4.1g | Cholesterol: 0mg | Sodium: 168.8mg

INGREDIENTS

- 1/4 cup chopped onion
- 2 cloves garlic, minced
- 2 tablespoons vegetable oil
- 3 cups uncooked instant rice (such as Minute)
- 2 1/4 cups chicken broth
- 1 cup vegetable juice (such as V8)
- 1 1/2 teaspoons taco seasoning

DIRECTIONS

1. Cook and stir onion, garlic, and vegetable oil in a skillet over medium heat until onions are softened, about 5 minutes.

2. Stir rice into onion mixture and cook, stirring often, until rice becomes slightly opaque, 1 to 2 minutes.
3. Stir chicken broth, vegetable juice, and taco seasoning into rice mixture and bring to a boil. Cover and simmer over low heat until rice has absorbed most of the liquid, about 5 minutes.

CORN AND RICE MEDLEY

Servings: 5 | Prep: 5m | Cooks: 25m | Total: 30m

NUTRITION FACTS

Calories: 262.9 | Carbohydrates: 50.4g | Protein: 5.7g | Cholesterol: 12.2mg | Sodium: 36.3mg

INGREDIENTS

- 2 tablespoons butter, divided
- 1 cup Basmati rice
- 2 cups water
- 2 cups fresh corn kernels
- 3 eaches large shallots, sliced thinly
- 1/2 teaspoon white sugar
- salt to taste
- ground black pepper to taste
- 2 tablespoons chopped fresh mint leaves

DIRECTIONS

1. Melt 1 tablespoon butter in a small saucepan over medium heat. Stir in the rice, add the water, and bring to a boil. Reduce heat, cover and simmer for 16 to 18 minutes, or until water is absorbed and rice is tender.
2. Meanwhile, melt 1 tablespoon butter in a large skillet over medium heat. Stir in corn, shallots, sugar, salt and pepper. Cook, stirring occasionally, for 4 to 6 minutes, or until tender.
3. In a serving bowl combine cooked rice, corn mixture and mint.

JAMAICAN RICE

Servings: 2 | Prep: 15m | Cooks: 30m | Total: 45m

NUTRITION FACTS

Calories: 398.3 | Carbohydrates: 71.6g | Protein: 6.1g | Cholesterol: 0mg | Sodium: 11.1mg

INGREDIENTS

- 1 tablespoon vegetable oil
- 2/3 cup brown rice

- 1/2 large onion, sliced
- 1/2 red apple, cored and sliced
- 1 pinch curry powder
- 1 cup water
- 1 teaspoon dark molasses or treacle
- 1 small banana, sliced
- 1 tablespoon unsweetened flaked coconut

DIRECTIONS

1. Heat the oil in a saucepan over medium heat. Add the onion and red apple; cook and stir until onion is transparent. Season with curry powder, and stir in the water. Add the rice and molasses, cover, and cook over low heat until the rice is tender, and water has been absorbed, about 30 minutes.
2. Mix in the banana, then sprinkle the coconut on top. Heat through for a moment over low heat before serving.

SUNNY PEPPER PARMESAN RICE WITH SPINACH

Servings: 8 | Prep: 15m | Cooks: 15m | Total: 30m

NUTRITION FACTS

Calories: 224.9 | Carbohydrates: 30.1g | Protein: 5.1g | Cholesterol: 5.5mg | Sodium: 942.8mg

INGREDIENTS

- 2 cups uncooked instant rice
- 2 cups water
- 1 tablespoon vegetable oil
- 1 large orange bell pepper, finely chopped
- 1 cup red bell pepper, finely chopped
- 1 cup yellow bell pepper, finely chopped
- 3 tablespoons chopped sweet onion
- 2 cups torn baby spinach leaves
- 1 teaspoon garlic salt
- 1 tablespoon seasoned salt
- 1 cup vinaigrette salad dressing to taste
- 1/2 cup grated Parmesan cheese

DIRECTIONS

1. Place rice and water in a pot, and bring to a boil. Let sit five minutes. Fluff with a fork.
2. Heat the oil in a wok over medium heat. Stir in the orange bell pepper, red bell pepper, yellow bell pepper, onion, and spinach. Season with garlic salt and seasoned salt. Cook 5 minutes. Mix in cooked rice, vinaigrette and Parmesan cheese. Continue cooking until heated through.

CAJUN WILD RICE

Servings: 6 | Prep: 10m | Cooks: 45m | Total: 55m

NUTRITION FACTS

Calories: 247.7 | Carbohydrates: 21.2g | Protein: 9.1g | Cholesterol: 23.6mg | Sodium: 988.9mg

INGREDIENTS

- 1 cup uncooked wild rice
- 1 (14 ounce) can chicken broth
- 1/4 cup water
- 1/2 pound andouille sausage, diced
- 1/2 cup diced sweet onion
- 1 cup chopped fresh mushrooms
- 1 tablespoon minced garlic
- 1 (10.75 ounce) can condensed cream of mushroom soup

DIRECTIONS

1. In a saucepan, combine the wild rice, chicken broth, water, sausage, onion, mushrooms and garlic. Bring to a boil, then reduce heat to low, cover, and simmer for 25 to 30 minutes, or until rice is tender. Remove from the heat, and stir in the cream of mushroom soup. It's that easy!

APPLE SPICE RICE

Servings: 6 | Prep: 10m | Cooks: 20m | Total: 30m

NUTRITION FACTS

Calories: 328.2 | Carbohydrates: 58.7g | Protein: 4.5g | Cholesterol: 22.9mg | Sodium: 67.2mg

INGREDIENTS

- 3 tablespoons butter
- 1 cup long grain rice
- 1/2 cup finely chopped onion
- 1 clove garlic, minced
- 1 small tart apple - peeled, cored and diced
- 1/2 cup golden raisins
- 1 1/2 cups chicken broth

DIRECTIONS

1. Melt butter in a saucepan over medium heat. Stir in rice, onion, garlic, apple and raisins. Saute for 3 to 4 minutes. Stir in chicken broth, and bring to a boil. Reduce heat, cover, and simmer for 16 to 18 minutes, or until liquid is absorbed.

INDONESIAN SPICED RICE

Servings: 8 | Prep: 25m | Cooks: 25m | Total: 35m

NUTRITION FACTS

Calories: 226.2 | Carbohydrates: 39.8g | Protein: 3.7g | Cholesterol: 0mg | Sodium: 3.9mg

INGREDIENTS

- 3 tablespoons vegetable oil
- 1 large onion, chopped
- 2 jalapeno peppers, seeded and minced
- 2 cloves garlic, crushed
- 1 teaspoon ground turmeric
- 1/2 teaspoon ground cinnamon
- 2 cups uncooked long-grain white rice
- 2 (14.5 ounce) cans chicken broth
- 1 cup water
- 1 bay leaf
- 2 green onions, chopped

DIRECTIONS

1. Heat oil in large, heavy pan over medium heat. Stir in onion, jalapeno peppers and garlic. Saute until onion is translucent; about 8 minutes.
2. Stir turmeric, cinnamon, and rice into the pan; stir for 2 minutes. Mix in the chicken broth, water and bay leaf. Bring the mixture to a boil, reduce heat to low, cover and cook 20 minutes.
3. Turn off the heat altogether and let sit for 5 minutes. Garnish with chopped green onion.

BETTER SPANISH RICE

Servings: 4 | Prep: 10m | Cooks: 10m | Total: 20m

NUTRITION FACTS

Calories: 164.2 | Carbohydrates: 28g | Protein: 3.6g | Cholesterol: 0mg | Sodium: 165.7mg

INGREDIENTS

- 1 tablespoon vegetable oil
- 1/2 onion, chopped
- 1 1/4 cups uncooked instant rice
- 1 (14.5 ounce) can diced tomatoes
- 1/2 cup chopped fresh cilantro
- 1 cup chicken broth

DIRECTIONS

1. Heat the oil in a skillet over medium-high heat, and cook and stir the chopped onion until browned, about 8 minutes.
2. Stir in the rice, tomatoes, cilantro, and chicken broth, and bring to a boil. Reduce the heat to medium-low, and simmer until the rice is cooked and most of the liquid is absorbed, about 10 minutes.

MATAR PULAO (RICE WITH PEAS)

Servings: 6 | Prep: 5m | Cooks: 25m | Total: 30m

NUTRITION FACTS

Calories: 312.7 | Carbohydrates: 58.7g | Protein: 6.7g | Cholesterol: 0mg | Sodium: 63.4mg

INGREDIENTS

- 2 tablespoons vegetable oil
- 4 eaches whole cloves
- 3 eaches black cardamom seeds
- 6 eaches whole black peppercorns
- 2 (3 inch) cinnamon sticks
- 2 teaspoons garlic powder
- 2 tablespoons water
- 1 cup frozen green peas, thawed
- 2 cups uncooked basmati rice, rinsed and drained
- 4 cups water
- 1 pinch salt to taste

DIRECTIONS

1. Heat the oil in a deep heavy skillet over low heat. Add the cloves, cardamom seeds, peppercorns and cinnamon sticks. Cook for a few minutes to bring out the aroma of the spices. Stir the garlic powder and 2 tablespoons of water together to make a paste; mix into the pan with the spices.
2. Add the green peas to the pan, cover and cook for about 5 minutes.

3. Add the remaining 4 cups of water and rice to the pan. Season with a little salt. Bring to a boil, then cover, and cook for about 15 minutes, until the rice is tender and the water has been absorbed. Taste, and adjust the salt before serving.

FRESH TASTING BLACK BEANS WITH RICE

Servings: 2 | Prep: 20m | Cooks: 5m | Total: 25m

NUTRITION FACTS

Calories: 272.1 | Carbohydrates: 60g | Protein: 5.8g | Cholesterol: 0mg | Sodium: 5.7mg

INGREDIENTS

- 3/4 cup uncooked white rice
- 2 cups water
- 1 (15 ounce) can black beans; drain and reserve liquid
- 2 tablespoons lemon juice
- 1 tablespoon garlic powder
- 1 1/2 teaspoons dried cilantro

DIRECTIONS

1. Bring a medium size pot of water to a boil, add rice. Bring back to a boil, then reduce heat to simmer. Let rice simmer 15-20 minutes, until tender.
2. Place beans and rice in a medium size saucepan. Heat over a medium heat, stirring frequently. Stir in reserved bean liquid as needed. Remove pan from heat and stir in lemon juice, garlic powder and cilantro. Let sit a moment, and stir in fresh oregano. Serve immediately.

RICE WITH ALMONDS AND RAISINS

Servings: 4 | Prep: 5m | Cooks: 20m | Total: 25m

NUTRITION FACTS

Calories: 261.8 | Carbohydrates: 44.6g | Protein: 5.6g | Cholesterol: 9.5mg | Sodium: 382.5mg

INGREDIENTS

- 1 tablespoon butter
- 1/3 cup finely chopped onion
- 1 cup uncooked white rice
- 1 1/2 cups chicken broth
- salt and pepper to taste
- 1/4 cup sliced almonds

- 2 tablespoons raisins

DIRECTIONS

1. Melt butter in a medium saucepan over medium heat. Saute onion, stirring, until tender. Stir in the rice, raisins, broth, salt and pepper. Bring to a boil.
2. Reduce heat to low, cover and simmer 15 to 20 minutes, or until rice is cooked and liquid is absorbed. Stir in almonds before serving.

SAUTEED RICE WITH KALE

Servings: 6 | Prep: 15m | Cooks: 20m | Total: 35m

NUTRITION FACTS

Calories: 320.7 | Carbohydrates: 52.8g | Protein: 5.4g | Cholesterol: 5.1mg | Sodium: 28.3mg

INGREDIENTS

- 1 cup chopped kale
- 3 tablespoons olive oil
- 1 tablespoon butter
- 1 small onion, diced
- 1 stalk celery, diced
- 1/2 cup sliced fresh mushrooms
- 1/2 green bell pepper, diced
- 2 cloves garlic, minced
- 2 cups cooked white rice
- 1 teaspoon dry mustard
- 2 pinches cayenne pepper
- 1 pinch salt and ground black pepper to taste

DIRECTIONS

1. Place a steamer insert into a saucepan and fill with water to just below the bottom of the steamer. Bring the water to a boil. Add the kale, cover, and steam until just tender, 7 to 10 minutes.
2. Heat olive oil and butter in a large skillet over medium heat; cook and stir onion, celery, mushrooms, green bell pepper, and garlic in the oil and butter mixture until the onion is tender, about 5 minutes. Stir kale and rice into the mixture, breaking the rice into grains with your spoon as you stir; season with dry mustard, cayenne pepper, salt, and black pepper. Cook and stir until the rice is hot, about 5 minutes.

AWESOME RICE PILAF

Servings: 8 | Prep: 20m | Cooks: 25m | Total: 55m | Additional: 10m

NUTRITION FACTS

Calories: 366.2 | Carbohydrates: 71.1g | Protein: 8.3g | Cholesterol: 11.4mg | Sodium: 379.5mg

INGREDIENTS

- 3 tablespoons butter
- 2 carrots, finely chopped
- 2 stalks celery, finely chopped
- 1 small red bell pepper, diced
- 1 small onion, finely chopped
- 4 cloves garlic, minced
- 3 cups white rice
- 1 (8.75 ounce) can no-salt-added sweet corn, drained
- 1 (15 ounce) can no-salt-added sweet peas, drained
- 5 1/2 cups chicken broth
- 1 1/2 tablespoons soy sauce
- 1 1/2 tablespoons Worcestershire sauce
- 2 teaspoons lemon pepper
- 2 teaspoons dried crushed parsley
- 4 pinches dried crushed thyme
- 1 pinch saffron
- 1 pinch salt and ground black pepper to taste

DIRECTIONS

1. Melt butter in a large saucepan over medium heat; cook and stir carrots, celery, red bell pepper, onion, and garlic until the vegetables begin to soften, about 5 minutes.
2. Gently stir rice, corn, and peas into vegetables to combine. Pour chicken broth, soy sauce, and Worcestershire sauce into rice mixture. Season with lemon pepper, parsley, thyme, saffron, salt, and black pepper, bring to a boil, and reduce heat to low. Cover and simmer until rice is tender, about 20 minutes. Remove from heat and let pilaf stand covered until grains are separate, 10 to 15 more minutes.

SWEET BELL PEPPER RICE

Servings: 4 | Prep: 15m | Cooks: 35m | Total: 50m

NUTRITION FACTS

Calories: 238 | Carbohydrates: 42.4g | Protein: 4.6g | Cholesterol: 1.1mg | Sodium: 76.9mg

INGREDIENTS

- 2 cups water
- 1 cup long grain rice
- 1 tablespoon olive oil
- 1 small sweet onion, finely chopped
- 3 cloves garlic, minced
- 1 small green bell pepper, chopped
- 1 small red bell pepper, chopped
- 1 teaspoon dried basil
- 1 teaspoon dried oregano
- 1/2 teaspoon ground black pepper
- 1 tiny pinch salt
- 1 splash dry white wine
- 1 tablespoon grated Parmesan cheese

DIRECTIONS

1. Bring water and rice to a boil in a saucepan. Reduce heat to medium-low, cover, and simmer until the rice is tender and liquid has been absorbed, 20 to 25 minutes.
2. Heat oil in a large skillet over medium-high heat. Cook and stir onion in the hot oil until tender, about 3 minutes. Add garlic and continue to cook and stir until onion is translucent, 2 to 3 minutes more. Stir green bell pepper and red bell pepper into onion mixture; cook until tender, about 5 minutes. Season with basil, oregano, black pepper, and salt.
3. Pour wine into vegetable mixture and reduce heat to medium low. Simmer until liquid is reduced, about 5 minutes. Stir rice into vegetables. Top with Parmesan cheese before serving.

A HOMEMADE SAN FRANCISCO TREAT: CHICKEN VERMICELLI RICE

Servings: 4 | Prep: 5m | Cooks: 30m | Total: 35m

NUTRITION FACTS

Calories: 223.5 | Carbohydrates: 42.4g | Protein: 4.5g | Cholesterol: 7.8mg | Sodium: 310.7mg

INGREDIENTS

- 1 tablespoon butter
- 1 cup white rice
- 1/4 cup broken pieces vermicelli pasta
- 1 tablespoon chicken bouillon granules
- 2 teaspoons dried parsley
- 1/4 teaspoon garlic powder

- 3 cups water
- 1/4 teaspoon onion powder

DIRECTIONS

1. Melt butter in a large saucepan over medium heat. Cook rice and vermicelli in hot butter until browned, about 3 minutes.
2. Pour water over the rice mixture. Stir chicken bouillon, parsley, garlic powder, and onion powder into the water; bring to a boil, place a cover on the saucepan, reduce heat to low, and cook until the water has absorbed into the rice and pasta, about 25 minutes.

MUSHROOM ONION RICE

Servings: 4 | Prep: 5m | Cooks: 30m | Total: 35m

NUTRITION FACTS

Calories: 275.6 | Carbohydrates: 47G | Protein: 6.1g | Cholesterol: 2.9mg | Sodium: 825.8mg

INGREDIENTS

- 2 tablespoons margarine
- 1 cup long-grain white rice
- 1 (10.5 ounce) can condensed French onion soup
- 1 (4 ounce) can canned mushrooms, drained
- 2 cups water

DIRECTIONS

1. Melt margarine in a saucepan over medium heat. Stir in rice and cook just until lightly browned. Mix in soup, mushrooms and water. Bring to a boil. Reduce heat to low, cover and simmer 25 minutes.

RICE-AH-RONI

Servings: 6 | Prep: 10m | Cooks: 28m | Total: 38m

NUTRITION FACTS

Calories: 297 | Carbohydrates: 51.4g | Fat: 6.7g | Protein: 6.8g | Cholesterol: 18mg | Sodium: 1098mg

INGREDIENTS

- 1 1/2 teaspoons kosher salt, plus more as needed
- 1/8 teaspoon freshly ground black pepper
- 1/8 teaspoon cayenne pepper
- 3 tablespoons unsalted butter

- 1/8 teaspoon ground coriander
- 1/8 teaspoon mustard powder
- 1/8 teaspoon celery salt
- 1/8 teaspoon paprika
- 1/8 pinch ground turmeric
- 1/2 cup finely diced onions
- 2/3 cup uncooked orzo pasta
- 1 1/3 cups uncooked long-grain white rice
- 3 cups good-quality chicken broth
- 1 tablespoon freshly chopped parsley

DIRECTIONS

1. Mix together salt, pepper, coriander, mustard powder, celery salt, paprika, turmeric, and cayenne pepper in a small bowl.
2. Melt butter in a large skillet over medium-high heat. Add diced onion and pasta. Cook and stir until onions soften and pasta turns golden brown, 4 to 6 minutes. Stir in spice blend; cook and stir about 30 seconds. Add rice and stir until rice is coated with butter, about 1 minute.
3. Pour in chicken broth. Bring to a simmer. Stir; reduce heat to low. Cover with a tight-fitting lid; cook for 17 minutes. Remove from heat; let covered skillet sit for 5 minutes. Remove lid and stir in parsley, fluffing rice and breaking up any clumps.

PERSIAN SABZI POLO (HERB RICE WITH FAVA BEANS)

Servings: 16 | Prep: 20m | Cooks: 55m | Total: 1H15m

NUTRITION FACTS

Calories: 233.8 | Carbohydrates: 44.7g | Protein: 5.5g | Cholesterol: 0mg | Sodium: 0mg

INGREDIENTS

- 6 cups water
- 4 cups uncooked long-grain white rice
- 3 tablespoons vegetable oil
- 1/2 cup water
- 1 bunch fresh dill, chopped
- 1 bunch fresh parsley, chopped
- 1 bunch fresh cilantro, chopped
- 2 cups fresh or frozen fava beans
- ground turmeric to taste
- ground cinnamon to taste
- 1 teaspoon salt
- 1 teaspoon pepper

DIRECTIONS

1. In a large saucepan bring water to a boil. Rinse rice; stir into boiling water. Boil just until rice rises to the surface of the water. Drain rice and return it to the saucepan. Stir in the oil and water. Mix in the dill, parsley, cilantro, fava beans, turmeric, cinnamon, salt and pepper.
2. Cook the rice over medium heat for 5 minutes.
3. Reduce heat to the lowest setting. Cover and simmer for 40 to 45 minutes. Note: It's normal to end up with crispy rice (called Tadig) on the bottom of the pot after cooking; it's delicious.

BOK CHOY STEAMED RICE

Servings: 4 | Prep: 10m | Cooks: 25m | Total: 35m

NUTRITION FACTS

Calories: 191 | Carbohydrates: 39.7g | Fat: 1.2g | Protein: 5.1g | Cholesterol: 0mg | Sodium: 210mg

INGREDIENTS

- 1 large head bok choy
- 1 1/2 cups cold water
- 1 cup long grain rice
- 1 teaspoon soy sauce
- 1 teaspoon chili-garlic sauce (such as sambal)
- 1/2 teaspoon sesame oil
- 1/4 teaspoon toasted sesame seeds

DIRECTIONS

1. Separate bok choy leaves from stems. Slice stems into 1-inch pieces; chop leaves.
2. Combine water, rice, and soy sauce in a pot; bring to a simmer and stir in bok choy stems. Reduce heat to low, cover the pot with a lid, and cook until rice is almost cooked through, about 18 minutes.
3. Stir bok choy leaves, chili-garlic sauce, and sesame oil into rice mixture with a fork. Remove pot from heat, cover the pot with a lid, and let sit until rice is cooked through and bok choy leaves wilt, about 5 minutes more. Fluff with a fork and garnish with sesame seeds.

RICE ELENA

Servings: 8 | Prep: 10m | Cooks: 30m | Total: 40m

NUTRITION FACTS

Calories: 465.1 | Carbohydrates: 21.1g | Protein: 19.7g | Cholesterol: 88.7mg | Sodium: 746.8mg

INGREDIENTS

- 1 tablespoon butter, or as needed
- 3 cups cooked rice, or more to taste
- 2 cups sour cream
- 1 pound shredded Monterey Jack cheese
- 2 (4 ounce) cans chopped green chilies
- 1/2 cup grated Cheddar cheese
- 1 pinch salt to taste

DIRECTIONS

1. Preheat oven to 350 degrees F (175 degrees C). Butter a 2-quart casserole dish.
2. Mix rice, sour cream, Monterey jack cheese, green chiles, and salt together in the prepared casserole dish. Sprinkle Cheddar cheese over the rice mixture.
3. Bake in preheated oven until hot in the center, about 30 minutes.

ONE BOWL RICE

Servings: 8 | Prep: 15m | Cooks: 45m | Total: 1h

NUTRITION FACTS

Calories: 325.2 | Carbohydrates: 43.8g | Protein: 5.3g | Cholesterol: 43.8mg | Sodium: 844.6mg

INGREDIENTS

- 2 cups uncooked long-grain rice
- 1 (4.5 ounce) can mushrooms, with liquid
- 2 stalks celery, finely chopped
- 1 red bell pepper, finely chopped
- 1 (1 ounce) package dry onion soup mix
- 1 (10.5 ounce) can beef broth
- 1/2 cup vegetable oil
- 1 cup water
- 3 tablespoons soy sauce

DIRECTIONS

1. Preheat oven to 350 degrees F (175 degrees C).
2. In a 9x13 inch baking dish, combine rice, mushrooms, celery, red bell pepper, onion soup mix, beef broth, oil, water and soy sauce.
3. Bake, covered, in preheated oven for 45 minutes, or until all liquid is absorbed and rice is cooked.

PERUVIAN CILANTRO RICE

Servings: 6 | Prep: 15m | Cooks: 20m | Total: 35m

NUTRITION FACTS

Calories: 189.9 | Carbohydrates: 27.3g | Protein: g11.8 | Cholesterol: 22mg | Sodium: 43.3mg

INGREDIENTS

- 2 (4 ounce) skinless, boneless chicken breast halves
- 1 bunch fresh cilantro, stems removed
- 1/2 cup water
- 1 tablespoon vegetable oil
- 1 tablespoon minced garlic
- 1/4 cup frozen, chopped carrots
- 1/4 cup frozen peas
- 1 tablespoon cumin
- 1 pinch salt and freshly ground black pepper to taste
- 1 cup uncooked white rice

DIRECTIONS

1. Place the chicken into a large saucepan and fill with enough water to cover, about 3 cups. Bring to a boil and cook for about fifteen minutes, or until chicken is done. Dice chicken, and reserve cooking liquid.
2. In a food processor or blender, puree cilantro with 1/2 cup water.
3. Heat oil in a saucepan and cook garlic until lightly browned. Pour in 2 cups of the cooking liquid and stir in the cilantro puree, diced chicken, carrots, peas, cumin and rice. Season with salt and pepper to taste. Bring to a simmer, then cover; cook on low heat until rice is tender and liquid has been absorbed, 15 to 20 minutes.

BAHAMIAN STYLE PEAS AND RICE

Servings: 4 | Prep: 20m | Cooks: 1h10m | Total: 1h30m

NUTRITION FACTS

Calories: 547.9 | Carbohydrates: 80.7g | Protein: 13.6g | Cholesterol: 40.2mg | Sodium: 746.3mg

INGREDIENTS

- 1/4 cup butter
- 2 ounces sliced bacon,
- 1 tablespoon ketchup
- 1 pinch salt and pepper to

diced

taste

- 1 large onion, diced
- 1 stalk celery, diced
- 1 large tomato, diced
- 1/2 (6 ounce) can tomato paste

- 1 (15 ounce) can pigeon peas, with liquid
- 1 2/3 cups water
- 1 1/2 cups uncooked long-grain white rice
- 1 sprig fresh thyme, chopped

DIRECTIONS

1. Melt butter in a large, heavy saucepan over medium high heat. Place bacon in the saucepan, and cook until evenly brown. Stir in onion and celery, and cook until tender. Mix in tomato, tomato paste, and ketchup. Season with salt and pepper. Reduce heat to low, and continue cooking about 15 minutes.
2. Melt butter in a large, heavy saucepan over medium high heat. Place bacon in the saucepan, and cook until evenly brown. Stir in onion and celery, and cook until tender. Mix in tomato, tomato paste, and ketchup. Season with salt and pepper. Reduce heat to low, and continue cooking about 15 minutes.

MUSHROOMS AND PEAS RICE

Servings: 5 | Prep: 10m | Cooks: 15m | Total: 25m

NUTRITION FACTS

Calories: 269 | Carbohydrates: 41.2g | Protein: 9.2g | Cholesterol: 11.4mg | Sodium: 492.6mg

INGREDIENTS

- 8 ounces fresh mushrooms, sliced
- 1 tablespoon butter
- 1 (10.75 ounce) can condensed cream of mushroom soup

- 10 3/4 fluid ounces milk
- 1 3/4 cups instant rice
- 1 1/2 cups frozen green peas

DIRECTIONS

1. In a large skillet, saute mushrooms in butter. Set aside.
2. Warm condensed cream of mushroom soup and milk. When it comes to a slow bubble, add instant rice and cover. Let sit for at least 5 minutes.

3. While the soup mixture is warming, thaw the peas in the microwave at 30 second intervals. Do not overheat the peas.
4. When the rice is tender, stir mushrooms and peas into the rice and season with salt and pepper to taste.

SIMPLE SPICED RICE

Servings: 8 | Prep: 5m | Cooks: 25m | Total: 30m

NUTRITION FACTS

Calories: 195.6 | Carbohydrates: 38g | Protein: 3.7g | Cholesterol: 7.6mg | Sodium: 605.8mg

INGREDIENTS

- 2 tablespoons butter
- 2 cups uncooked basmati rice
- 1 small onion, chopped
- 4 cups water
- 2 teaspoons salt
- 2 eaches whole cinnamon sticks
- 1 large bay leaf

DIRECTIONS

1. Melt the butter in a large saucepan over medium heat, and cook and stir the basmati rice and onion until the rice kernels are coated with butter and the onion is translucent, 5 to 8 minutes. The rice will give off a slightly toasted fragrance. Pour in water, and mix in salt, cinnamon sticks and bay leaf.
2. Bring the mixture to a boil, and reduce heat to medium-low. Cover the saucepan, and simmer the rice until all the water has disappeared and the rice appears dry, about 18 minutes. Fluff the rice with a fork and serve.

REALLY SIMPLE RICE

Servings: 6 | Prep: 10m | Cooks: 25m | Total: 40m | Additional: 5m

NUTRITION FACTS

Calories: 149.3 | Carbohydrates: 26.9g | Protein: 3.6g | Cholesterol: 1.3mg | Sodium: 93.7mg

INGREDIENTS

- 1 tablespoon olive oil
- 1 cup long-grain white
- 2 cups low-sodium chicken broth
- 1 pinch garlic salt, or to

rice

taste

- 1/2 small onion, finely diced

DIRECTIONS

1. Heat olive oil in a non-stick saucepan over medium-high heat nearly to smoking. Cook and stir rice in the hot oil quickly to toast the rice, 2 to 3 minutes. Stir the onion into the rice; cook and stir 1 minute more. Pour chicken broth over the rice mixture, season with garlic salt, and bring to a boil; reduce heat to low, place a cover on the saucepan, and cook until the broth is absorbed and the rice is tender, about 20 minutes. Remove from heat and allow to rest 5 minutes before lifting the lid.

RICE PATTIES

Servings: 4 | Prep: 10m | Cooks: 10m | Total: 50m | Additional: 30m

NUTRITION FACTS

Calories: 134.2 | Carbohydrates: 12.8g | Protein: 4.6g | Cholesterol: 53.9mg | Sodium: 207.9mg

INGREDIENTS

- 1 cup cooked rice
- 1/2 small onion, chopped
- 1/4 cup shredded Cheddar cheese
- 1 egg, beaten
- 1 teaspoon minced garlic
- 1/4 teaspoon salt
- 1/4 teaspoon red pepper flakes
- 1/4 teaspoon ground black pepper, or more to taste
- 1/4 teaspoon chopped fresh parsley, or to taste
- 1 pinch onion powder, or to taste
- 1 tablespoon vegetable oil, or more to taste

DIRECTIONS

1. Mix rice, onion, Cheddar cheese, egg, garlic, salt, red pepper flakes, black pepper, parsley, and onion powder by hand in a bowl.
2. Cover bowl with plastic wrap and refrigerate at least 30 minutes.
3. From rice mixture into 4 small patties.
4. Heat vegetable oil in a large skillet over medium-high heat. Fry patties in hot oil until lightly browned, about 5 minutes per side.

JEERA (CUMIN) RICE

Servings: 2 | Prep: 5m | Cooks: 15m | Total: 20m

NUTRITION FACTS

Calories: 464.9 | Carbohydrates: 77g | Protein: 6.5g | Cholesterol: 0mg | Sodium: 0.9mg

INGREDIENTS

- 2 tablespoons vegetable oil
- 1/2 teaspoon cumin seeds
- 1 cup dry jasmine rice
- 1 3/4 cups water
- salt to taste

DIRECTIONS

1. Heat the oil in a medium size saucepan over a medium-high heat. Drop in the cumin seeds, and cook until they splutter. Do not allow the cumin seeds to burn or become really dark brown in color. Add the rice and fry it in the oil for about 1 minute.
2. Add the water and salt and bring to a boil. Once the water is boiling, reduce the heat to low and cover the saucepan. Cook the rice for approximately 15 minutes. If you feel the rice is getting burnt near the base of the pan as it cooks, one trick is to place the saucepan on another flat pan or griddle which is directly on the flame. Toss with a fork.

DOLMAS (STUFFED GRAPE LEAVES)

Servings: 8 | Prep: 30m | Cooks: 45m | Total: 1h15m

NUTRITION FACTS

Calories: 207.4 | Carbohydrates: 39.1g | Protein: 5.3g | Cholesterol: 0mg | Sodium: 846.7mg

INGREDIENTS

- 1 tablespoon olive oil
- 2 onions, minced
- 1 1/2 cups uncooked white rice
- 2 tablespoons tomato paste
- 2 tablespoons dried currants
- 1 tablespoon ground cinnamon
- 1 tablespoon dried mint
- 1 tablespoon dried dill weed
- 1 teaspoon ground allspice
- 1 teaspoon ground cumin

- 2 tablespoons pine nuts
- 1 (8 ounce) jar grape leaves, drained and rinsed

DIRECTIONS

1. Heat oil in a medium saucepan over medium heat. Saute onions until tender. Stir in rice and hot water to cover. Cover and simmer until rice is half cooked, about 10 minutes.
2. Remove from heat and stir in tomato paste, currants, pine nuts, cinnamon, mint leaves, dill weed, allspice and cumin. Let mixture cool.
3. Prepare a large pot by placing an inverted plate on the bottom; this protects the dolmas from direct heat when steaming.
4. Rinse grape leaves in warm water; drain and cut off any stems. Place about 1 teaspoon of the cooled rice mixture in the center of a leaf. Fold in the sides and then roll into a cigar shape. Place in prepared pot. Repeat with remaining ingredients.
5. Pour in just enough warm water to reach the bottom of the first layer of dolmas. Cover and simmer over low heat for 30 to 45 minutes, or until rice is totally cooked. Check the water level often and add more as necessary.

CARROTS AND RICE

Servings: 12 | Prep: 15m | Cooks: 40m | Total: 55m

NUTRITION FACTS

Calories: 284.9 | Carbohydrates: 36.3g | Protein: 3.3g | Cholesterol: 38mg | Sodium: 513.6mg

INGREDIENTS

- 1 cup sliced carrots
- 2 cups uncooked long grain white rice
- 3 tablespoons minced onion
- 1/2 cup white sugar
- 4 1/2 cups water
- 1 cup half-and-half cream
- 2 teaspoons salt
- 3/4 cup butter

DIRECTIONS

1. In a large saucepan, combine carrots, onion, water, and salt. Bring to a boil, reduce heat to medium, and simmer for 10 minutes. Stir in rice. Reduce heat to low, and cover pan. Allow to steam for 20 minutes.
2. Stir sugar, half-and-half, and butter into rice mixture. Consistency should be creamy, not dry. Stir in some milk if necessary. Remove from heat, and serve immediately.

REBECCA'S WILD RICE PILAF

Servings: 15 | Prep: 20m | Cooks: 1h30m | Total: 1h50m

NUTRITION FACTS

Calories: 169.7 | Carbohydrates: 18.7g | Protein: 4.5g | Cholesterol: 17mg | Sodium: 283mg

INGREDIENTS

- 1 serving cooking spray
- 1/2 cup butter
- 1 cup uncooked wild rice
- 3/4 cup uncooked brown rice
- 6 eaches green onions, chopped
- 1 (8 ounce) package sliced mushrooms
- 1 (2.25 ounce) package slivered almonds
- 1 (10.5 ounce) can condensed French onion soup
- 1 (10.5 ounce) can beef consomme

DIRECTIONS

1. Preheat an oven to 350 degrees F (175 degrees C). Spray a 2 quart stove top and oven-safe baking dish with nonstick cooking spray.
2. Melt butter in the baking dish over medium heat. Stir in the wild rice and brown rice. Cook and stir for 5 minutes. Stir in the onions; cook for 5 additional minutes. Remove from heat. Stir in the mushrooms and almonds. Pour onion soup and consomme over the rice mixture. Cover with lid or aluminum foil that has been coated with nonstick cooking spray.
3. Bake until rice is tender and the liquid has been absorbed, about 1 hour and 15 minutes. Stir before serving.

INDIAN RICE PILAF

Servings: 4 | Prep: 10m | Cooks: 20m | Total: 30m

NUTRITION FACTS

Calories: 187.6 | Carbohydrates: 40.1g | Protein: 4.1g | Cholesterol: 2.3mg | Sodium: 440.1mg

INGREDIENTS

- 1/4 cup water
- 1 (14.5 ounce) can chicken broth
- 1/4 teaspoon ground cinnamon
- 1/8 teaspoon paprika

- 1 cup long grain rice
- 1 teaspoon curry powder
- 1/2 teaspoon garlic powder
- 2 pinches ground cloves
- 1 small onion, coarsely chopped

DIRECTIONS

1. Bring water and chicken broth to a boil.
2. Combine rice, curry powder, garlic powder, cinnamon, paprika, and cloves in a bowl; stir to mix. Add spiced rice and onion to the boiling broth. Cover and cook until rice is tender, 20 to 25 minutes.

CHICKENY CHICKENY RICE

Servings: 4 | Prep: 5m | Cooks: 25m | Total: 30m

NUTRITION FACTS

Calories: 370.3 | Carbohydrates: 62.4g | Protein: 6.4g | Cholesterol: 15.6mg | Sodium: 620.2mg

INGREDIENTS

- 3 cups water
- 2 cubes chicken bouillon
- 1 tablespoon olive oil
- 1 large onion, chopped
- 2 tablespoons butter
- 1
- 1/2 cups uncooked white rice
- salt and pepper to taste

DIRECTIONS

1. Preheat oven to 450 degrees F (230 degrees C).
2. In a medium saucepan heat water and bullion to a slow boil over medium-high heat. In a large oven safe skillet, heat oil over medium heat. Saute onions until transparent. Increase heat to high and add butter and rice. Stir constantly until the rice becomes starchy, about 3 minutes, and then carefully pour the chicken bouillon stock into the skillet.
3. Place the skillet in the oven and bake for 20 minutes. Season with salt and pepper to taste.

HONEY RICE

Servings: 6 | Prep: 20m | Cooks: 15m | Total: 35m

NUTRITION FACTS

Calories: 333.5 | Carbohydrates: 65.8g | Protein: 6.1g | Cholesterol: 18.3mg | Sodium: 72.1mg

INGREDIENTS

- 3 cups cooked rice
- 1/2 cup raisins
- 2 1/2 cups milk
- 1/2 cup honey
- 2 tablespoons butter
- 1 teaspoon grated lemon rind
- 1 tablespoon lemon juice
- 1/8 teaspoon ground cinnamon

DIRECTIONS

1. Combine rice, raisins, milk, honey, and butter in a saucepan. Bring the mixture to a boil, reduce the heat, and let it simmer for 15 minutes; stirring occasionally. Stir in lemon rind and juice.
2. Serve the rice in bowls and garnish (optional) with cinnamon and slivered almonds.

CHARLESTON RED RICE

Servings: 8 | Prep: 15m | Cooks: 1h5m | Total: 1h20m

NUTRITION FACTS

Calories: 330.6 | Carbohydrates: 51.9g | Protein: 8.1g | Cholesterol: 14.3mg | Sodium: 1387.7mg

INGREDIENTS

- 2 cups uncooked long-grain white rice
- 6 cups boiling water
- 1 tablespoon salt
- 6 slices bacon
- 2 eaches onions, chopped
- 1 (8 ounce) can tomato sauce
- 1 (6 ounce) can tomato paste
- 1 tablespoon white sugar
- 2 teaspoons Worcestershire sauce
- 1 dash hot pepper sauce

DIRECTIONS

1. Preheat oven to 325 degrees F (165 degrees C). Grease a 2-quart baking dish.
2. Bring the rice, water, and salt to a boil in a saucepan. Reduce heat to medium-low, cover, and simmer until the rice is tender and most of the liquid has been absorbed, 20 to 25 minutes.
3. While the rice is cooking, cook the bacon in a large, deep skillet over medium-high heat until evenly browned, about 10 minutes. Reserve about 1 tablespoon of bacon drippings in the pan. Reduce heat to medium. Drain the bacon on a plate lined with paper towels; crumble the bacon once cooled enough to handle.
4. Cook and stir the onions in the reserved bacon drippings until translucent, 5 to 8 minutes. Stir in the crumbled bacon, tomato sauce, tomato paste, sugar, Worcestershire sauce, and hot sauce; bring the mixture to a simmer, reduce heat, and simmer for 10 minutes. Spoon the cooked rice into the prepared baking dish and stir the tomato-bacon mixture into the rice until evenly combined.
5. Cover the dish and bake in the preheated oven for 45 minutes.

SPANISH BROWN RICE

Servings: 4 | Prep: 10m | Cooks: 50m | Total: 1h10m | Additional: 10m

NUTRITION FACTS

Calories: 198.6 | Carbohydrates: 42.2g | Protein: 5g | Cholesterol: 0mg | Sodium: 396.3mg

INGREDIENTS

- 1 cup brown rice
- 1 teaspoon minced garlic
- 2 cups water
- 1 cup salsa
- 1 cup diced tomatoes

DIRECTIONS

1. Combine rice and garlic in a saucepan. Stir in water, salsa, and diced tomatoes. Bring to a boil.
2. Stir rice mixture and reduce heat to low. Simmer, covered, for 50 minutes. Turn off heat and allow rice to sit, covered, for an additional 5 to 10 minutes. Stir rice before serving.

MEXICAN VEGETABLE RICE

Servings: 6 | Prep: 5m | Cooks: 10m | Total: 15m

NUTRITION FACTS

Calories: 263.9 | Carbohydrates: 48g | Protein: 6g | Cholesterol: 0mg | Sodium: 762.8mg

INGREDIENTS

- 2 tablespoons canola oil
- 1 cup diced onion
- 2 teaspoons minced garlic
- 1 1/2 cups white rice
- 1 1/2 teaspoons salt
- 3/4 teaspoon cayenne pepper

- 3 cups vegetable stock
- 1 (10 ounce) package frozen mixed peas and carrots, thawed
- 1 1/2 cups tomatoes, deseeded and diced
- 2 tablespoons chopped fresh parsley
- 2 green onions, chopped

DIRECTIONS

1. In a large saute pan, saute onion, garlic, and rice in canola oil until onion is soft and rice is opaque. Add salt, cayenne pepper, and vegetable stock to the pan. Bring the liquid to a boil. Cover the pan and reduce heat to low, simmer for 20 minutes or until all of the liquid is absorbed.
2. Add vegetables and tomatoes. Cover pan and allow to sit for 5 minutes. Turn off heat. Sprinkle top of rice with parsley and green onions.

FANTASTIC GREEN RICE DISH

Servings: 5 | Prep: 5m | Cooks: 1h50m | Total: 1h55m

NUTRITION FACTS

Calories: 346.1 | Carbohydrates: 37g | Protein: 11.3g | Cholesterol: 116.5mg | Sodium: 201.8mg

INGREDIENTS

- 1 cup uncooked white rice
- 1/2 cup shredded Cheddar cheese
- 1 small onion, grated
- 2 eggs, beaten

- 1/4 cup butter, softened
- 1 cup fresh parsley
- 1 1/2 cups milk

DIRECTIONS

1. Preheat oven to 250 degrees F (120 degrees C).

2. In a saucepan bring 2 cups of water to a boil. Add rice and stir. Reduce heat, cover and simmer for 20 minutes.
3. To the cooked rice add cheese, onion, eggs and butter. Mix well and gently stir in parsley and milk. Transfer to a 2 quart casserole dish.
4. Bake in preheated oven for 1 1/2 hours.

CHEESY CONFETTI RICE

Servings: 6 | Prep: 10m | Cooks: 40m | Total: 50m

NUTRITION FACTS

Calories: 274.3 | Carbohydrates: 28.6g | Protein: 7.6g | Cholesterol: 37.1mg | Sodium: 300.5mg

INGREDIENTS

- 1/4 cup butter
- 1 cup uncooked long-grain rice
- 1/4 cup chopped onion
- 2 1/2 cups water
- 1 (4 ounce) can diced green chiles, drained
- 1 tablespoon chicken bouillon
- 1 cup shredded Monterey Jack cheese
- 1/4 cup sliced ripe olives
- 1/2 (4 ounce) jar diced pimento peppers, drained
- 2 tablespoons chopped fresh parsley

DIRECTIONS

1. In a 2 quart saucepan over medium heat melt butter and stir in rice and onion. Cook over medium heat, stirring constantly, until rice turns golden brown, about 8 to 10 minutes.
2. Slowly add water, green chiles and chicken bouillon. Bring mixture to a boil, reduce heat and cover. Simmer until rice is tender, about 25 to 30 minutes. Stir in cheese, olives, pimientos and parsley.

ORANGE RICE

Servings: 4 | Prep: 5m | Cooks: 5m | Total: 10m

NUTRITION FACTS

Calories: 223.8 | Carbohydrates: 44.9g | Protein: 4.2g | Cholesterol: 7.6mg | Sodium: 29mg

INGREDIENTS

- 1 teaspoon grated orange zest
- 1 1/2 cups instant rice

- 1 1/2 cups orange juice
- 1 tablespoon butter
- 1 (11 ounce) can mandarin orange segments, drained

DIRECTIONS

1. In a saucepan over medium-high heat, combine the orange zest, orange juice, and butter. Bring to a boil, and stir in rice. Cover, and remove from heat. Let stand 5 minutes. Mix in mandarin orange segments, and serve immediately.

INDIAN RICE (PULAO)

Servings: 16 | Prep: 30m | Cooks: 40m | Total: 1h10m

NUTRITION FACTS

Calories: 266.6 | Carbohydrates: 44.7g | Protein: 4.9g | Cholesterol: 0.9mg | Sodium: 306.6mg

INGREDIENTS

- 1/4 teaspoon saffron threads or ground turmeric
- 6 cups boiling water
- 1/2 cup vegetable shortening
- 2 medium onions, chopped
- 2 (1 inch) pieces cinnamon stick
- 4 eaches whole cloves
- 1 teaspoon ground ginger
- 2 tablespoons ground cumin
- 1 teaspoon garlic powder
- 10 cardamom seeds
- 4 1/2 cups long-grain white rice
- 1 cup plain yogurt
- 2 teaspoons salt

DIRECTIONS

1. Place saffron threads into boiling water, set aside to steep.
2. Melt the vegetable shortening in a large pot over medium-high heat. Stir in the onions, and cook until golden, about 5 minutes. Season with cinnamon sticks, cloves, ginger, cumin, garlic powder, and cardamom seeds. Cook for 3 to 4 minutes to release the flavor, stirring constantly.
3. Pour in the rice and cook for 10 minutes, stirring constantly. Add the yogurt, saffron water, and salt. Bring to a simmer, then reduce heat to low. Cover pot with a cloth folded into 4 layers. Place a lid

over the cloth and cook until the rice is done, about 20 minutes. Remove the cinnamon sticks, cloves, and cardamom seeds before serving.

BAKED "FRIED" RICE

Servings: 6 | Prep: 20m | Cooks: 40m | Total: 1h10m

NUTRITION FACTS

Calories: 361 | Carbohydrates: 56.9g | Fat: 9.9g | Protein: 9.8g | Cholesterol: 14mg | Sodium: 1351mg

INGREDIENTS

- 2 cups long-grain white rice
- 2 tablespoons canola oil
- 1 tablespoon sesame oil, or to taste
- 3 cloves garlic, crushed
- 1/2 cup sliced green onions
- 1/2 cup diced red bell peppers
- 1/2 cup diced carrots
- 1/2 cup green peas
- 1 cup diced ham
- 1 pinch salt to taste (optional)
- 3 cups chicken broth
- 3 tablespoons soy sauce
- 2 teaspoons chile paste (optional)

DIRECTIONS

1. Preheat the oven to 400 degrees F (200 degrees C).
2. Place rice in a large baking dish. Drizzle in canola and sesame oils; toss to coat rice completely. Add garlic, green onions, bell peppers, carrots, peas, and ham. Season with salt. Stir until well combined.
3. Combine chicken broth, soy sauce, and chile paste in a pot over high heat. Stir and bring to a boil. Pour on top of the rice and stir briefly. Cover top tightly with heavy-duty aluminum foil.
4. Bake in the preheated oven for 32 minutes. Remove and let stand for 10 minutes. Uncover; fluff rice with a fork. Taste and adjust seasoning.
5. Increase oven temperature to 475 degrees F (245 degrees C). Return to the oven until rice is browned and crusted, about 10 minutes.

GREEN RICE

Servings: 6 | Prep: 10m | Cooks: 25m | Total: 35m

NUTRITION FACTS

Calories: 319 | Carbohydrates: 59.7g | Protein: 7g | Cholesterol: 1.7mg | Sodium: 370.4mg

INGREDIENTS

- 2 tablespoons olive oil
- 2 bunches green onions, sliced, white parts and tops separated
- 2 jalapeno peppers, seeded and minced
- 2 tablespoons sherry
- 2 cups uncooked long-grain rice
- salt to taste
- 1 teaspoon black pepper
- 2 cups chicken broth
- 1 1/2 cups water
- 1/2 cup minced cilantro
- 1/2 cup minced parsley

DIRECTIONS

1. Heat olive oil in a large skillet over medium heat. Saute the white parts of the green onions with the jalapenos for 5 minutes; do not brown.
2. Stir in the sherry, rice, salt and pepper. Pour in the broth and water; bring to a boil. Cover, reduce heat to low, and cook until rice is tender and liquid is absorbed, about 20 minutes.
3. Fluff with a fork and stir in cilantro, parsley and tops of green onions. Transfer to a warm serving dish and serve immediately.

EASY HERB RICE

Servings: 4 | Prep: 10m | Cooks: 15m | Total: 25m

NUTRITION FACTS

Calories: 170.3 | Carbohydrates: 37.8g | Protein: 3.5g | Cholesterol: 0.1mg | Sodium: 116.6mg

INGREDIENTS

- 2 cups water
- 1 teaspoon instant beef bouillon granules
- 2 teaspoons dried minced onion
- 1/2 teaspoon dried thyme
- 1/2 teaspoon dried marjoram
- 1/4 teaspoon dried rosemary
- 1 cup white rice

DIRECTIONS

1. Mix water, beef bouillon, onion, thyme, marjoram, and rosemary together in a saucepan; bring to a boil. Add rice, reduce heat to medium-low, cover, and simmer until water is absorbed and rice is tender, 15 to 20 minutes.

TASTY SPICY RICE PILAF

Servings: 4 | Prep: 20m | Cooks: 15m | Total: 35m

NUTRITION FACTS

Calories: 287.4 | Carbohydrates: 49.8g | Protein: 6.5g | Cholesterol: 15.8mg | Sodium: 937.4mg

INGREDIENTS

- 2 tablespoons butter
- 1 onion, diced
- 1 roasted red pepper, diced
- 6 mushrooms, chopped
- 6 cloves garlic, minced
- 2 cups uncooked instant rice
- 3 cups chicken stock
- 2 teaspoons red pepper flakes
- 1/2 teaspoon salt
- 1/2 teaspoon ground black pepper

DIRECTIONS

1. Melt butter in a large pot over medium heat; cook and stir onion, red pepper, mushrooms, and garlic until tender, about 10 minutes. Stir in rice. Add chicken stock; cover and boil until liquid is absorbed, about 10 minutes. Season with red pepper flakes, salt, and black pepper.

CUBAN-STYLE YELLOW RICE

Servings: 24 | Prep: 10m | Cooks: 20m | Total: 30m

NUTRITION FACTS

Calories: 119.8 | Carbohydrates: 26.1g | Protein: 2.6g | Cholesterol: 0mg | Sodium: 205.6mg

INGREDIENTS

- 4 cups long grain rice
- 8 cups water
- 1/8 teaspoon paprika
- 1 pinch black pepper to taste

- 1 small onion, minced

- 2 teaspoons salt

- 1/8 teaspoon annatto powder

- 1 cup frozen peas, thawed

- 1 (4 ounce) jar sliced pimento peppers, for garnish

DIRECTIONS

1. Place the rice in a sieve and rinse under cold water until the water runs clear. Shake sieve to remove excess water from rice.
2. Place rice in a large saucepan with a tightly fitting lid and add water. Stir in the onion, salt, annatto powder, paprika, and pepper. Bring the mixture to a boil over medium-high heat. Reduce heat to low, cover pan, and simmer. After cooking for 10 minutes, gently stir the peas into the rice. Cook until all the water is evaporated and the rice is tender, 15 to 20 minutes longer. Serve garnished with pimento slices.

PEANUT RICE

Servings: 4 | Prep: 10m | Cooks: m | Total: 30m

NUTRITION FACTS

Calories: 302.2 | Carbohydrates: 45.7g | Protein: 9g | Cholesterol: 0mg | Sodium: 318.4mg

INGREDIENTS

- 1 cup uncooked basmati rice
- 2 1/4 cups water
- 1/2 teaspoon salt

- 1/4 teaspoon ground turmeric
- 1/2 cup frozen petite peas, thawed
- 1/2 cup dry roasted peanuts

DIRECTIONS

1. Mix the rice, water, salt, and turmeric in a pot, and bring to a boil. Cover, reduce heat to low, and simmer 20 minutes.
2. Stir the peas and peanuts into the cooked rice to serve.

EASY BACON FRIED RICE

Servings: 4 | Prep: 20m | Cooks: 15m | Total: 35m

NUTRITION FACTS

Calories: 271.2 | Carbohydrates: 37.7g | Protein: 9.6g | Cholesterol: 58.3mg | Sodium: 793.3mg

INGREDIENTS

- 6 slices bacon, cut into 1/2-inch pieces
- 1 cup frozen French-cut green beans, thawed
- 1/2 onion, roughly chopped
- 2 cloves garlic, minced
- 2 teaspoons sesame oil
- 1 egg, beaten
- 3 cups cold cooked rice
- 1 tablespoon soy sauce, or more to taste

DIRECTIONS

1. Place bacon in a large, deep skillet and cook over medium-high heat, turning occasionally, until just beginning to brown, about 7 minutes. Drain all but 1 to 2 teaspoons of bacon grease from the skillet. Add green beans, onion, and garlic; saute until bacon is crisp and green beans and onions are softened, about 3 minutes.
2. Push bacon mixture to one side of the skillet; heat sesame oil on the empty side, about 30 seconds. Pour in egg; cook until just set, about 1 minute. Stir into bacon mixture to combine. Mix in rice. Stir in soy sauce, a tablespoon at a time, until rice is evenly coated. Cook until rice is heated through, 3 to 5 minutes.

BLACK RICE

Servings: 4 | Prep: 5m | Cooks: 35m | Total: 40m

NUTRITION FACTS

Calories: 266.1 | Carbohydrates: 38.2g | Protein: 5.2g | Cholesterol: 15.4mg | Sodium: 296.5mg

INGREDIENTS

- 2 tablespoons butter
- 1 cup black rice
- 1/4 cup diced onion
- 1/4 cup slivered almonds
- 1 3/4 cups water
- 1 cube chicken bouillon

DIRECTIONS

1. Melt butter in a saucepan over medium heat. Add black rice, onion, and almonds; cook and stir until lightly toasted, 5 to 10 minutes. Add water and bouillon cube; bring to a boil. Reduce hear to low, cover, and simmer until rice is tender and liquid is absorbed, 25 to 30 minutes.

WILD RICE WITH ROSEMARY AND CASHEW STUFFING
Servings: 4 | Prep: 5m | Cooks: 20m | Total: 25m

NUTRITION FACTS

Calories: 301.2 | Carbohydrates: 31g | Protein: 8.1g | Cholesterol: 0.3mg | Sodium: 846.9mg

INGREDIENTS

- 1 teaspoon olive oil
- 1/2 cup onion, chopped
- 1/2 cup chopped fresh mushrooms
- 1 cup chopped cashews
- 1 tablespoon chopped fresh rosemary
- 1 3/4 cups chicken stock
- 1 cup long grain and wild rice mix

DIRECTIONS

1. Heat oil in a skillet over medium heat. Saute onions until tender and translucent. Stir in mushrooms, and saute until soft. Add rosemary, and cook for 1 minute. Stir in cashews, and cook for 1 minute. Transfer to a medium saucepan.
2. Pour in chicken stock, and stir in rice. Cover, and bring to a boil. Reduce heat, and simmer until water is absorbed. Remove from heat, and let stand for 5 minutes. Stuff into the cavity of a small roasting chicken.

GRANDMA'S RICE
Servings: 4 | Prep: 10m | Cooks: 1h5m | Total: 1h15m

NUTRITION FACTS

Calories: 421.3 | Carbohydrates: 43.7g | Protein: 8.8g | Cholesterol: 62.1mg | Sodium: 815.6mg

INGREDIENTS

- 2 (4 ounce) cans mushroom stems and pieces, undrained
- 1 small white onion, chopped

- 1 (10.5 ounce) can condensed beef consomme (such as Campbell's ®)
- 1/2 cup water
- 1 cup white rice
- 1 stick butter, cut into 4 pieces
- 2 teaspoons garlic powder
- 1 tablespoon grated Parmesan cheese

DIRECTIONS

1. Preheat an oven to 350 degrees F (175 degrees C).
2. Stir the mushrooms with juice, beef consomme, water, rice, and onion together in a glass baking dish with a lid. Arrange the butter atop the rice. Season with the garlic powder. Cover with lid.
3. Bake in the preheated oven for 1 hour. Sprinkle the Parmesan cheese over the top and return to the oven until the cheese melts slightly, about 5 minutes.

KICKIN' RICE

Servings: 6 | Prep: 10m | Cooks: 25m | Total: 35m

NUTRITION FACTS

Calories: 82.6 | Carbohydrates: 13g | Protein: 1.9g | Cholesterol: 1.7mg | Sodium: 756.8mg

INGREDIENTS

- 1 tablespoon vegetable oil
- 1 cup long-grain white rice
- 1 (4 ounce) can chopped green chilies
- 1 teaspoon ground black pepper
- 2 cups chicken broth

DIRECTIONS

1. Heat vegetable oil in a saucepan over medium heat. Stir rice in hot oil until coated; add green chiles and continue cooking until rice begins to brown lightly, 2 to 3 minutes. Season rice with pepper. Pour broth into the saucepan; bring to a boil. Reduce heat to low, place cover on the saucepan, and cook until the broth is absorbed and the rice tender, about 20 minutes.

DOLMATHES

Servings: 7 | Prep: 45m | Cooks: 45m | Total: 1h30m

NUTRITION FACTS

Calories: 534.6 | Carbohydrates: 55.3g | Protein: 7.4g | Cholesterol: 0mg | Sodium: 935mg

INGREDIENTS

- 1 cup olive oil, divided
- 1 1/2 pounds onions, chopped
- 1 3/4 cups uncooked white rice
- 2 lemons, juiced
- 2 tablespoons chopped fresh dill
- 1/2 cup chopped fresh parsley
- 2 tablespoons pine nuts
- 1 (8 ounce) jar grape leaves, drained and rinsed

DIRECTIONS

1. Preheat oven to 375 degrees F (190 degrees C).
2. Heat 2 tablespoons oil in a large saucepan over medium heat. Saute onions until tender. Stir in rice and brown slightly. Add 3 1/2 cups water, and half of the lemon juice. Reduce heat, cover and simmer for 20 minutes, or until all liquid is absorbed and rice is tender. Stir in dill, parsley and pine nuts.
3. Remove stems from grape leaves and place 1 tablespoon of rice mixture in the center. Fold in the sides and roll tightly. Place, folded side down, in a baking dish and cover with remaining olive oil, lemon juice and enough water to cover 1/2 of the dolmathas.
4. Cover with aluminum foil and bake in preheated oven for 45 minutes.

COLORADO MEXICAN RICE

Servings: 6 | Prep: 20m | Cooks: 20m | Total: 40m

NUTRITION FACTS

Calories: 359.3 | Carbohydrates: 40g | Protein: 8.9g | Cholesterol: 22mg | Sodium: 301.2mg

INGREDIENTS

- 2 cups water
- 1 cup uncooked white rice
- 4 medium tomatoes, halved
- 2 carrots, chopped
- 1 small potato, peeled and chopped
- 1/2 cup sour cream

- 1/2 medium onion
- 1 clove garlic, peeled
- 1/4 cup olive oil
- 1/2 cup fresh shelled green peas
- 1 bunch fresh cilantro, chopped
- 1 serrano pepper, chopped
- salt to taste
- 4 ounces manchego cheese

DIRECTIONS

1. Preheat oven to 450 degrees F (230 degrees C). Lightly grease a medium baking sheet.
2. Bring water to boil in a medium saucepan, and stir in rice. Reduce heat, cover, and simmer for 20 minutes.
3. Place tomato halves, onion, and garlic in a single layer on the prepared baking sheet. Stirring occasionally, roast 10 to 15 minutes in the preheated oven, until evenly browned. Remove from heat, and allow to cool completely.
4. Puree the roasted vegetables in a blender or food processor. Drain any remaining liquid from rice.
5. Heat olive oil in a medium skillet over medium heat. Stir in serrano chili, and cook until tender. Place rice, pureed vegetables, peas, carrots, potato, and sour cream in the skillet. Season with cilantro and salt. Cook and stir until all vegetables are tender and rice is browned. Mix in manchego cheese to melt before serving.

CORN AND RICE

Servings: 5 | Prep: 20m | Cooks: 50m | Total: 1h10m

NUTRITION FACTS

Calories: 421.8 | Carbohydrates: 92g | Protein: 10.7g | Cholesterol: 2mg | Sodium: 1119.7mg

INGREDIENTS

- 1 slice bacon, chopped
- 1/2 onion, chopped
- 1/4 green bell pepper, chopped
- 1/2 teaspoon chopped fresh thyme
- 1/2 cup tomato sauce
- 1 teaspoon browning sauce
- 1 teaspoon salt
- 1/2 teaspoon ground black pepper
- 1 pinch red pepper flakes
- 2 (14 ounce) cans whole kernel corn, drained
- 3 1/2 cups water
- 2 cups white rice

DIRECTIONS

1. Cook the bacon in a large saucepan over medium heat until the grease begins to render. Stir in the onion, bell pepper, and thyme; cook until the onion is nearly translucent. Reduce heat to medium-low and add the tomato sauce, browning sauce, salt, black pepper, and red pepper flakes; stir; simmer another 3 minutes. Add the corn; simmer another 3 minutes. Slowly pour the water into the mixture while stirring. Raise the heat to high and stir in the rice; bring to a boil; cover and reduce heat to low. Simmer until the rice has absorbed all the moisture, about 30 minutes; fluff with a fork to serve.

GREEN LENTILS AND RICE ASSYRIAN STYLE

Servings: 8 | Prep: 10m | Cooks: 30m | Total: 40m

NUTRITION FACTS

Calories: 234.5 | Carbohydrates: 34.6g | Protein: 8.2g | Cholesterol: 0mg | Sodium: 222.1mg

INGREDIENTS

- 1 cup dry green lentils
- 2 cups water
- 4 tablespoons olive oil, divided
- 1 cup basmati rice
- 1 large onion, chopped
- 3/4 teaspoon salt, or to taste

DIRECTIONS

1. Place the lentils into a pot and cover with the water. Bring to a rolling boil over high heat for 5 minutes, then cover and remove from heat. Meanwhile, rinse the rice in cold water until water comes out clear.
2. Heat 2 tablespoons olive oil or vegetable oil in a skillet over medium heat. Stir in the rice for about 1 minute, until the grains turn opaque and white, then stir in the lentils and water. Bring the rice mixture to a boil, then cover and reduce heat to medium-low for 5 minutes. Stir once, then cover and reduce heat further to low. Continue cooking, covered (don't remove the lid!) until the rice is tender, about 15 minutes more.
3. Meanwhile, heat the remaining 2 tablespoons of oil in the skillet over medium heat. Stir in the onion; cook and stir until the onion has softened and turned translucent, about 5 minutes. Reduce heat to medium-low, and continue cooking and stirring until the onion is very tender and dark brown, 15 to 20 minutes more. When the rice is ready, stir in the caramelized onion and season with salt.

SIMPLE BAKED RICE

Servings: 4 | Prep: 15m | Cooks: 45m | Total: 1h

NUTRITION FACTS

Calories: 218.6 | Carbohydrates: 40.2g | Protein: 4.2g | Cholesterol: 2.5mg | Sodium: 495.1mg

INGREDIENTS

- 1 serving cooking spray
- 1 cup long-grain rice
- 1 tablespoon olive oil
- 1/4 cup diced carrot
- 1/4 cup diced celery
- 1/4 cup diced onion
- 2 cloves garlic, minced
- 2 cups chicken stock
- 1 bay leaf
- 1 pinch ground black pepper, or to taste

DIRECTIONS

1. Preheat oven to 350 degrees F (175 degrees C). Prepare a 2-quart casserole dish with cooking spray.
2. Spread long-grain rice into prepared casserole dish.
3. Heat olive oil in a saucepan over medium heat. Cook and stir carrot, celery, and onion in hot oil until onion is soft and translucent, about 4 minutes. Stir garlic into mixture; cook and stir 1 minute more. Increase heat to high; add chicken stock and bay leaf to the saucepan and bring to a boil. Pour the mixture over the rice in the casserole dish. Cover the dish tightly with aluminum foil.
4. Bake in preheated oven 20 minutes. Remove aluminum foil and continue baking until the rice is tender and has absorbed most of the liquid, about 20 minutes more. Remove and discard bay leaf; season with black pepper. Fluff with a fork to serve.

LEMONGRASS COCONUT RICE

Servings: 6 | Prep: 5m | Cooks: 30m | Total: 35m

NUTRITION FACTS

Calories: 186.7 | Carbohydrates: 14.3g | Protein: 2.8g | Cholesterol: 0mg | Sodium: 226.6mg

INGREDIENTS

- 1 stalk lemongrass, bottom 6 inches only, outer leaves peeled
- 1 cup long-grain rice, rinsed and drained
- 2 eaches bay leaves
- 1/2 teaspoon ground turmeric

- 1 3/4 cups coconut milk
- 1 pinch salt

DIRECTIONS

1. Lightly pound the lemongrass stalk with a kitchen mallet. Combine the lemongrass, rice, coconut milk, bay leaves, turmeric, and salt in a saucepan over medium heat. Bring the mixture to a boil, stirring occasionally; reduce heat to low and simmer until all liquid is absorbed, about 25 minutes. Remove bay leaves and lemongrass before serving.

NON-BALAYA

Servings: 6 | Prep: 20m | Cooks: 1h15m | Total: 1h35m

NUTRITION FACTS

Calories: 737.2 | Carbohydrates: 54.4g | Protein: 38.9g | Cholesterol: 117.9mg | Sodium: 1241.4mg

INGREDIENTS

- 2 tablespoons vegetable oil
- 4 eaches skinless, boneless chicken breast halves - cubed
- 1/4 cup butter
- 1 onion, finely chopped
- 1/2 cup minced green onion
- 1 bunch fresh parsley, minced
- 1 1/2 teaspoons chopped garlic
- 5 cups chicken broth
- 1 (1 pound) package smoked sausage, quartered lengthwise and sliced
- 2 cups uncooked white rice

DIRECTIONS

1. Heat the vegetable oil in a large pot over medium-high heat. Cook the chicken until no longer pink in the center and the juices run clear, 3 to 5 minutes. Remove from pot and set aside.
2. Melt the butter in the large pot. Cook the onion, green onion, and parsley in the butter until the onions begin to soften, 4 to 7 minutes. Stir in the garlic and cook until brown, 3 to 4 minutes. Add the chicken broth, cooked chicken, sausage, and rice; bring to a boil for 2 minutes and then reduce heat to medium-low. Cover and simmer for 1 hour. Do not remove cover or stir while simmering. Serve hot.

MANGO-LIME RICE

Servings: 12 | Prep: 5m | Cooks: 50m | Total: 55m

NUTRITION FACTS

Calories: 123.2 | Carbohydrates: 26.3g | Protein: 2.5g | Cholesterol: 0mg | Sodium: 4.8mg

INGREDIENTS

- 2 cups brown rice
- 4 cups water
- 1 tablespoon fresh lime juice
- 1/2 cup chopped fresh cilantro
- 1 mango, peeled, pitted, and cut into 1/2 inch cubes

DIRECTIONS

1. Bring the brown rice and water to a boil in a saucepan. Stir the lime juice into the rice, reduce the heat to medium-low, and cover; simmer until the rice is tender and the liquid has been absorbed, 45 to 50 minutes.
2. Stir the cilantro and mango into the cooked rice to serve.

SEMI-INDULGENT EASY BROWN RICE

Servings: 4 | Prep: 10m | Cooks: 10m | Total: 20m

NUTRITION FACTS

Calories: 109.5 | Carbohydrates: 16.8g | Protein: 2.5g | Cholesterol: 8.3mg | Sodium: 23.7mg

INGREDIENTS

- 1 cup instant brown rice (such as Minute®)
- 1/2 teaspoon dried parsley
- 1/4 teaspoon ground black pepper
- 1 tablespoon unsalted butter
- 1/2 teaspoon lemon juice
- 7 fluid ounces low-sodium chicken broth, or more if needed

DIRECTIONS

1. Combine instant brown rice, parsley, and black pepper in a microwave-safe dish.
2. Place butter and lemon juice in a measuring cup.

3. Pour chicken broth into measuring cup with butter and lemon juice to measure a total of 1 cup.
4. Stir chicken broth mixture into rice mixture until all ingredients are moistened. Cover with microwave-safe lid.
5. Heat in the microwave oven until rice is tender and has absorbed the liquid, about 7 minutes.
6. Remove and let stand for 5 minutes. Fluff with fork before serving.

BROWN SPANISH RICE

Servings: 4 | Prep: 10m | Cooks: 1h | Total: 1h10m

NUTRITION FACTS

Calories: 156.3 | Carbohydrates: 32.3g | Protein: 4g | Cholesterol: 2.4mg | Sodium: 1478.8mg

INGREDIENTS

- 1 (14 ounce) can chicken broth
- 1 teaspoon salt
- 1 (15 ounce) can diced tomatoes with green chile peppers
- 1 cup brown rice

DIRECTIONS

1. Bring chicken broth, tomatoes, and salt to a boil in a medium saucepan; add rice. Cover, reduce heat to medium-low, and simmer until rice is cooked and liquid is absorbed, about 1 hour. Stir before serving.

QUICK SPANISH RICE

Servings: 6 | Prep: 15m | Cooks: 20m | Total: 35m

NUTRITION FACTS

Calories: 203.4 | Carbohydrates: 31.4g | Protein: 4.1g | Cholesterol: 15.4mg | Sodium: 606.6mg

INGREDIENTS

- 3 tablespoons butter
- 1 cup chopped onions
- 1 cup chopped green bell pepper
- 1/2 cup chopped celery
- 1 (28 ounce) can diced tomatoes with juice
- 2 teaspoons chili powder
- 2 teaspoons beef bouillon granules
- 1/2 teaspoon salt

- 1 clove garlic, minced
- 3 cups cooked white rice (such as Uncle Ben's®)

DIRECTIONS

1. Heat butter in a frying pan over medium heat; cook and stir onion, green bell pepper, celery, and garlic until slightly tender, 5 to 10 minutes. Stir tomatoes with juice, chili powder, beef bouillon granules, and salt into onion mixture; add rice. Simmer rice mixture, stirring occasionally, until heated through and flavors are blended, 15 to 20 minutes.

NO-FUSS PERFECT BAKED BROWN RICE

Servings: 6 | Prep: 5m | Cooks: 1h | Total: 1h5m

NUTRITION FACTS

Calories: 204.8 | Carbohydrates: 40.2g | Protein: 4g | Cholesterol: 0mg | Sodium: 198.9mg

INGREDIENTS

- 1 2/3 cups uncooked brown rice
- 2 1/2 cups boiling water
- 1/2 teaspoon salt
- 2 teaspoons canola oil

DIRECTIONS

1. Preheat oven to 350 degrees F (175 degrees C). Grease a 9x9 baking dish.
2. Place rice in prepared baking dish; sprinkle salt and oil on top. Pour boiling water over rice. Cover baking dish tightly with double layer of aluminum foil and pinch edges to seal.
3. Bake in center of preheated oven until water is absorbed, about 1 hour.
4. Remove rice from oven, uncover, and fluff with fork.

ASPARAGUS RISOTTO

Servings: 12 | Prep: 10m | Cooks: 40m | Total: 1h

NUTRITION FACTS

Calories: 178 | Carbohydrates: 26.6g | Fat: 5.1g | Protein: 4.9g | Cholesterol: 13mg

INGREDIENTS

- 1/4 cup LAND O LAKES® Butter
- 4 cups vegetable stock

- 2 tablespoons chopped shallots
- 1 (8 ounce) package fresh mushrooms, chopped
- 1 pound fresh asparagus, ends trimmed, cut into 1-inch pieces
- 1 1/2 cups uncooked Arborio rice
- 1/2 cup white wine
- 1 cup cherry tomatoes, halved
- 1/2 cup shredded Parmesan cheese
- 1/2 teaspoon freshly grated lemon zest
- Salt (optional)

DIRECTIONS

1. Melt butter in 4-quart saucepan over medium heat until sizzling. Add shallots, mushrooms and asparagus. Cook 4-5 minutes or until asparagus is crisply tender and shallots are softened. Remove vegetables from pan; set aside.
2. Place rice into pan; stir until well-coated. Cook 1 minute; add wine. Continue cooking, stirring occasionally, until wine is absorbed. Add stock 1/2 cup at a time, stirring occasionally after each addition, until liquid is absorbed.
3. Stir in cooked vegetables, cherry tomatoes, Parmesan cheese. Add lemon zest and salt, if desired.

CHRISTIAN RICE

Servings: 12 | Prep: 15m | Cooks: 45m | Total: 1h

NUTRITION FACTS

Calories: 222.6 | Carbohydrates: 18g | Protein: 9.2g | Cholesterol: 32.4mg | Sodium: 662.3mg

INGREDIENTS

- 1/2 cup converted long-grain white rice
- 1 (4.5 ounce) package dry noodle soup mix
- 4 1/2 cups water
- 1 pound bulk pork sausage
- 1 (10 ounce) package frozen chopped onion, thawed
- 1 red bell pepper, seeded and chopped
- 2 stalks celery, chopped
- 1 (3 ounce) package sliced almonds

DIRECTIONS

1. Preheat the oven to 400 degrees F (200 degrees C). In a large pot, combine the rice, both packets of soup mix and water. Bring to a boil, then simmer over low heat for 7 minutes.

2. Meanwhile, crumble the sausage into a large skillet over medium-high heat. As soon as it begins to release its juices, add the onion, pepper and celery. Cook and stir until sausage is browned and vegetables are tender. Drain, and stir into the rice mixture. The mixture will appear soupy, but the rice will absorb the liquid while baking. Pour into a greased 2 quart casserole dish. Cover with aluminum foil.

3. Bake for 30 minutes in the preheated oven. Remove the aluminum foil, sprinkle sliced almonds on top, and continue cooking for 15 minutes to let the top of the rice brown.

TUSCAN RISOTTO

Servings: 5 | Prep: 15m | Cooks: 25m | Total: 40m

NUTRITION FACTS

Calories: 272 | Carbohydrates: 41.2g | Fat: 8.1g | Protein: 7.2g | Cholesterol: 7mg | Sodium: 764mg

INGREDIENTS

- 2 tablespoons olive oil
- 1 large onion, minced
- 1 cup uncooked Arborio rice
- 1 (32 ounce) carton Swanson® Tuscan Chicken Flavor Infused Broth, heated
- 1/2 cup grated Parmesan cheese

DIRECTIONS

1. Heat the oil in a 4-quart saucepan over medium heat. Add the onion and cook for 3 minutes, stirring occasionally.

2. Stir the rice in the saucepan. Add 1/2 cup broth and cook and stir until it's absorbed. Add the remaining broth, 1/2 cup at a time, stirring until the broth is absorbed before adding more. Stir in the cheese before serving.

YELLOW RICE WITH VEGETABLES

Servings: 6 | Prep: 15m | Cooks: 30m | Total: 45m

NUTRITION FACTS

Calories: 205.8 | Carbohydrates: 42.8g | Protein: 4.4g | Cholesterol: 0mg | Sodium: 1243.9mg

INGREDIENTS

- 1 teaspoon vegetable oil
- 1 clove garlic, minced

- 1 small onion, chopped
- 1 carrot, diced
- 1/2 cup chopped broccoli florets
- 1/4 cup diced red bell pepper

- 3 cups vegetable broth
- 1 ½ cups rice
- 1 (1.41 ounce) package sazon seasoning with coriander and achiote (such as Goya®)
- 1 dash adobo seasoning with pepper (such as Goya®)

DIRECTIONS

1. Heat oil in a saucepan over medium heat. Cook and stir onion, carrot, broccoli, red bell pepper, and garlic in hot oil until garlic just begins to brown, about 5 minutes.
2. Pour vegetable broth into the saucepan; add rice, sazon seasoning, and adobo seasoning and stir. Bring the liquid to a boil, reduce heat to low, and cook until the liquid is absorbed and the rice is tender, about 25 minutes. Fluff rice with a fork to serve.

OUT OF THE HAT RICE

Servings: 4 | Prep: 10m | Cooks: 15m | Total: 35m | Additional: 10m

NUTRITION FACTS

Calories: 225.4 | Carbohydrates: 44.6g | Protein: 5.5g | Cholesterol: 7.6mg | Sodium: 59.8mg

INGREDIENTS

- 1 cup basmati rice, rinsed and drained
- 2 cups water
- 3 eaches green onions, chopped
- 1 pinch salt to taste

- 1 teaspoon cracked black pepper, or to taste
- 1 tablespoon butter
- 1 lemon, juiced
- 16 baby spinach leaves, divided

DIRECTIONS

1. Stir the basmati rice, water, green onions, salt, and pepper together in a saucepan over medium heat; bring to a boil. Stir in the butter. Reduce heat to low, cover the pan, and let simmer for 15 minutes. When the rice has steam openings in the top between the grains, stir in the lemon juice. Cover and let sit off the heat for 10 minutes to finish steaming.

2. To serve, place 4 spinach leaves in a fan shape on a plate; scoop up several balls of rice using an ice cream scoop. Place the rice scoops decoratively onto the spinach leaves, and serve.

SPICY AMERICAN SPANISH RICE

Servings: 8 | Prep: 15m | Cooks: 35m | Total: 50m

NUTRITION FACTS

Calories: 301.5 | Carbohydrates: 19.4g | Protein: 12.5g | Cholesterol: 59.7mg | Sodium: 697.2mg

INGREDIENTS

- 3 tablespoons butter
- 1 cup long-grain converted rice
- 1 green bell pepper, diced
- 1 onion, diced
- 1 pound ground beef
- 2 (15 ounce) cans tomato sauce
- 1 (14.5 ounce) can diced tomatoes with green chilies (such as ROTEL)

DIRECTIONS

1. Melt butter in a skillet over medium heat. Cook and stir rice in the melted butter until rice is lightly browned, 3 to 4 minutes. Stir bell pepper and onion into rice and cook until bell pepper is softened and onion is translucent, 5 to 8 minutes.
2. Break the ground beef into the rice mixture; cook and stir until beef is completely browned, 8 to 10 minutes. Stir tomato sauce and diced tomatoes into ground beef mixture. Cover, reduce heat, and simmer until rice is tender and liquid is absorbed, about 20 minutes.

RICE PILAF WITH RAISINS AND VEGGIES

Servings: 6 | Prep: 15m | Cooks: 25m | Total: 40m

NUTRITION FACTS

Calories: 268.4 | Carbohydrates: 50.5g | Protein: 4.8g | Cholesterol: 2.5mg | Sodium: 701.5mg

INGREDIENTS

- 3 cups chicken broth
- 2 tablespoons olive oil
- 3 cloves garlic, minced
- 1 teaspoon curry powder

- 4 stalks celery, chopped
- 1/2 large onion, diced
- 4 green onions, white and green parts separated and sliced
- 1/2 teaspoon salt
- 1 1/2cups uncooked white rice
- 1/2cup golden raisins

DIRECTIONS

1. Bring chicken broth to boil in a saucepan over medium-high heat; continue simmering while preparing remaining ingredients.
2. Heat olive oil in a large skillet over medium heat. Cook and stir celery, onion, green onion white portions, garlic, curry powder, and salt in the hot oil until vegetables are tender, about 5 minutes. Transfer vegetables to a bowl.
3. Cook and stir rice in the same skillet until lightly toasted, about 3 minutes.
4. Stir toasted rice into boiling chicken broth. Reduce heat to medium-low; continue simmering until rice is tender and broth is absorbed, about 15 minutes.
5. Remove rice from heat and stir in raisins, green onion tops, and celery mixture until well blended.

LEMON RICE WITH PEAS

Servings: 6 | Prep: 5m | Cooks: 25m | Total: 30m

NUTRITION FACTS

Calories: 232 | Carbohydrates: 40.4g | Fat: 5.1g | Protein: 5g | Cholesterol: 2mg | Sodium: 356mg

INGREDIENTS

- 1 1/2 cups uncooked long grain rice
- 1/4 teaspoon dried thyme
- 2 tablespoons margarine
- 1 (14.5 ounce) can chicken broth
- 1 1/4 cups water
- 1/4 cup ReaLemon lemon juice from concentrate
- 1/4 teaspoon pepper
- 3/4 cup frozen peas
- 2 tablespoons sliced almonds, toasted

DIRECTIONS

1. Cook and stir rice and thyme in hot margarine in medium-sized saucepan 5 minutes or until rice is lightly golden. Carefully stir in both, water, ReaLemon(R), and pepper. Bring to a boil. Reduce heat; cover and simmer 15 to 18 minutes or until rice is tender and liquid is absorbed.

2. Remove from heat. Stir in peas. Cover and let stand 5 minutes. Sprinkle with almonds. Optional: Top with garnish for added color.

GOLDEN RICE CAKES WITH SWEET POTATO-GINGER SAUCE

Servings: 6 | Prep: 15m | Cooks: 30m | Total: 1h | Additional: 15m

NUTRITION FACTS

Calories: 482 | Carbohydrates: 62.3g | Protein: 8.7g | Cholesterol: 62mg | Sodium: 435.6mg

INGREDIENTS

- 3 tablespoons canola oil
- 2 cloves garlic, minced
- 2 cups dry jasmine rice
- 2 1/2cups water
- 1 teaspoon salt
- 1 sweet potato
- 1 (14 ounce) can coconut milk
- 1/2cup orange juice
- 1 tablespoon minced fresh ginger root
- salt and pepper to taste
- 1 carrot, coarsely chopped
- 1/2 red bell pepper, chopped
- 4 green onions, chopped
- 2 eggs, beaten
- 2 green onions, thinly sliced

DIRECTIONS

1. In a saucepan with a tight-fitting lid heat 1 tablespoon of the canola oil with the garlic over medium heat for 1 minute, stirring constantly. Add the jasmine rice and stir constantly for 1 minute more. Add the 2-1/2 cups water and 1 teaspoon salt. Bring rice to a boil, then reduce the heat to low, cover the pan, and cook the rice for 15 minutes. Transfer the rice to a large bowl, and let it cool for 15 minutes.
2. While the rice cooks, cut the sweet potato into thirds. Place the pieces in a pot, and cover them with cold water. Bring the potatoes to a boil, and cook them until they are tender, about 20 minutes. Drain and let them cool.
3. In a saucepan bring the coconut milk, the water or orange juice, and the minced ginger almost to a boil, then turn the heat to low and cook for 5 minutes. Remove the pan from the heat.
4. Peel the skin off the cooled sweet potato. Puree the sweet potato flesh with the coconut-ginger liquid in a blender or food processor. Pour the sweet-potato puree back into the saucepan and add salt and pepper.

5. Mince the carrot, the red pepper, and the coarsely chopped scallions in a food processor. Add 1/2 of the jasmine rice and the 2 beaten eggs; run the machine in spurts until the mixture has a mealy consistency. Put this mixture back into the bowl with the rest of the jasmine rice and mix well. Put half of this mixture into a clean bowl.

6. Heat two skillets or a large griddle over medium-high heat. Divide the remaining canola oil between the skillets or spread it on the griddle. Divide the rice mixture in each bowl into thirds. Form each of the six parts into a ball then place each ball in a skillet or on the griddle. Pat the ball down to form a cake about 1 1/2 inches thick. Fry the cakes for 3 to 4 minutes per side, or until they are golden brown.

7. Reheat the sauce, and ladle it into plates. Place a rice cake on each plate, and top with the finely chopped scallions.

COCONUT SEVAI (RICE NOODLES)

Servings: 6 | Prep: 5m | Cooks: 15m | Total: 20m

NUTRITION FACTS

Calories: 370.4 | Carbohydrates: 48.1g | Protein: 5.2g | Cholesterol: 0mg | Sodium: 423.8mg

INGREDIENTS

- 14 ounces rice noodles
- 1 teaspoon salt
- 3 tablespoons vegetable oil
- 1 teaspoon black mustard seed
- 2 dried red chile peppers, chopped
- 3 tablespoons brown lentils
- 4 tablespoons roasted peanuts
- 3/4 cup shredded or flaked coconut
- 1/4 cup water
- fresh cilantro, for garnish

DIRECTIONS

1. Place noodles in a medium size pot and add water, just to cover. Add salt and bring to a boil. After boiling 1 to 2 minutes, transfer noodles to a colander and let cold water run through it for about 3 seconds. Drain and set aside.

2. Heat oil in a wok; when warm add mustard seed, chile peppers and lentils. Stir-fry until lentils start getting light brown, then add peanuts and stir-fry for 10 seconds. Stir in coconut and fry it until light brown; add cooked noodles and 1/4 cup water. Keep stirring all together over heat until well mixed, 10 to 20 seconds. Garnish with cilantro and serve.

JOSEPHINE'S PUERTO RICAN CHICKEN AND RICE

Servings: 6 | Prep: 10m | Cooks: 45m | Total: 1h | Additional: 5m

NUTRITION FACTS

Calories: 453.2 | Carbohydrates: 56.5g | Protein: 20.6g | Cholesterol: 52.1mg | Sodium: 621.7mg

INGREDIENTS

- 1 tablespoon vegetable oil
- 5 chicken drumsticks
- 1 small onion, chopped
- 1/2 cup pitted green olives
- 2 tablespoons capers
- 1 (8 ounce) can tomato sauce
- 3 tablespoons shortening
- 2 tablespoons achiote seed
- 4 cups boiling water
- 2 cups short-grain rice, rinsed

DIRECTIONS

1. In a large saucepan saute chicken, onions, olives and capers over medium heat. Pour in a little juice from the olives to add more olive flavor. As the onion begins to turn clear and the chicken begins to brown, add tomato sauce. Saute mixture until everything is lightly cooked. Reduce heat to low.
2. In a small saucepan melt shortening over medium heat; add achiote seeds. When the shortening turns red, remove it from the heat and strain out the seeds. Mix oil into chicken/tomato mixture. Add the boiling water to the mixture; increase the heat to medium high and bring to a boil, stirring well.
3. Add the rice to the boiling mixture and continue to boil for about 3 minutes. Reduce heat to low and continue cooking for about 30 minutes, or until rice is tender and has absorbed the liquid, stirring occasionally. Add more water if necessary (see Cook's Note). Remove from heat and let stand, covered, for 10 minutes.
4. Transfer mixture to a large bowl and serve immediately.

TURMERIC RICE WITH PEAS AND CARROTS

Servings: 6 | Prep: 5m | Cooks: 25m | Total: 30m

NUTRITION FACTS

Calories: 154.2 | Carbohydrates: 29.9g | Protein: 3.1g | Cholesterol: 5.2mg | Sodium: 222.9mg

INGREDIENTS

- 1 tablespoon butter
- 1 cube chicken bouillon

- 1 small onion, chopped
- 1 cup water
- 1 tablespoon ground turmeric
- 3/4 cup frozen mixed peas and carrots
- 1 cup white rice, rinsed

DIRECTIONS

1. Melt butter in a saucepan over medium heat. Add onion; cook and stir until golden, about 5 minutes. Add water, turmeric, and bouillon cube; stir well to combine. Add peas and carrots. Bring to a boil; stir in rice. Reduce heat and cook, covered, until rice is tender and liquid has been absorbed, about 15 minutes.

EASY LEMON RICE PILAF

Servings: 6 | Prep: 20m | Cooks: 28m | Total: 48m

NUTRITION FACTS

Calories: 281.9 | Carbohydrates: 40.2g | Protein: 6.3g | Cholesterol: 98mg | Sodium: 667.6mg

INGREDIENTS

- 2 large egg yolks
- 1/4 cup heavy whipping cream
- 2 tablespoons lemon juice
- 1 teaspoon lemon zest, or to taste
- 2 tablespoons butter
- 1 1/2 cups uncooked jasmine rice
- 3 cups chicken broth
- 1/4 cup grated Parmesan cheese
- 3 tablespoons chopped fresh parsley

DIRECTIONS

1. Combine egg yolks, cream, lemon juice, and lemon zest in a bowl; whisk thoroughly.
2. Melt butter in a saucepan over medium-high heat. Add rice; cook, stirring constantly, until opaque, 3 to 4 minutes. Add chicken broth; stir quickly. Bring to a boil. Reduce heat to low. Cover and simmer until rice is tender and liquid has been absorbed, 20 to 25 minutes.
3. Fold lemon-cream mixture into the rice; mix well. Stir in Parmesan cheese and parsley.

FESTIVE WILD RICE

Servings: 4 | Prep: 5m | Cooks: 20m | Total: 25m

NUTRITION FACTS

Calories: 184.4 | Carbohydrates: 40.1g | Protein: 6.2g | Cholesterol: 0mg | Sodium: 45.5mg

INGREDIENTS

- 1 (6 ounce) package uncooked wild rice
- 1/2 cup dried cranberries
- 1 cup frozen green peas, thawed

DIRECTIONS

1. Prepare rice according to package directions.
2. Microwave peas on high for 2 minutes, or until heated through.
3. Fold warm peas and cranberries into cooked rice.